FINDING PURPOSE

CHELSEA CANEDY

A Life Managing the Passion, Compulsion, and Borderline Addiction Called *Horses*

First published in 2025 by
Trafalgar Square Books | TrafalgarBooks.com
An Imprint of the Stable Book Group
32 Court Street, Suite 2109, Brooklyn, New York 11201

Copyright © 2025 Chelsea Canedy

All rights reserved. No part of this book may be reproduced, by any means, without written permission of the publisher, except by a reviewer quoting brief excerpts for a review in a magazine, newspaper, or website.

Disclaimer of Liability
The author and publisher shall have neither liability nor responsibility to any person or entity with respect to any loss or damage caused or alleged to be caused directly or indirectly by the information contained in this book. While the book is as accurate as the author can make it, there may be errors, omissions, and inaccuracies.

Some names and identifying details have been changed to protect the privacy of individuals.

Trafalgar Square Books encourages the use of approved safety helmets in all equestrian sports and activities.

Trafalgar Square Books certifies that the content in this book was generated by a human expert on the subject, and the content was edited, fact-checked, and proofread by human publishing specialists with a lifetime of equestrian knowledge. TSB does not publish books generated by artificial intelligence (AI).

Library of Congress Cataloging-in-Publication Data
Names: Canedy, Chelsea, author.
Title: Finding purpose : a life managing the passion, compulsion, and
   borderline addiction called "horses" / Chelsea Canedy.
Description: North Pomfret, Vermont : Trafalgar Square Books, 2025.
Identifiers: LCCN 2024051776 (print) | LCCN 2024051777 (ebook) | ISBN
   9781646012305 (paperback) | ISBN 9781646012312 (epub)
Subjects: LCSH: Canedy, Chelsea. | Horse trainers--Biography. |
   Human-animal relationships. | Horses--Social aspects.
Classification: LCC SF309.482.C36 A3 2025 (print) | LCC SF309.482.C36
   (ebook) | DDC 798.2092--dc23/eng/20250226
LC record available at https://lccn.loc.gov/2024051776
LC ebook record available at https://lccn.loc.gov/2024051777

Cover photograph by Kim Beaudoin/KTB Creative; interior photographs courtesy of Chelsea Canedy unless otherwise noted. In some cases, the photographers were not known; should additional photographers be identified, they will be credited in future editions of this book.

Book interior and cover design by RM Didier
Typefaces: Apparat, Cormorant

Printed in the United States of America

10 9 8 7 6 5 4 3 2 1

DEDICATION

*For everyone who has ever pondered
their place in this world
or their path in this lifetime.*

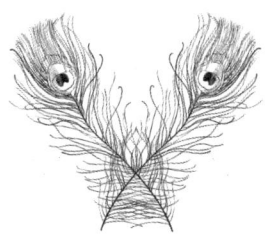

The peacock feather is often seen as a symbol of "the soul's journey toward enlightenment" and "encourages introspection, self-awareness, and a deeper connection to your higher self."

THE TIMES OF INDIA, AUGUST 9, 2024

INTRODUCTION
FINDING THE BEGINNING

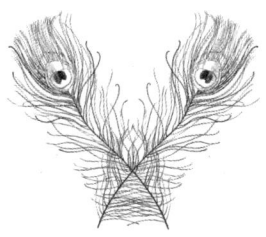

SOMEWHERE IN MY EARLY TWENTIES, I was home on a college break when my mom handed me a box of items from my childhood. Inside I found a thin, magazine-sized paperback workbook I had filled out at age six or seven. It was called *All About Me* and was full of prompts to answer questions about the things I liked and disliked at the time, and about what I imagined my future would hold. I smiled and chuckled quietly as I turned the pages and looked at the primitive drawings, faded snapshots, and messy handwriting that filled them. I flipped through slowly, reveling in the memories the book brought to the surface—how much I liked the color combination of red and purple, how straight and white-blonde my hair had been, how much I had loved every size and shape of animal.

Then I came upon a page that made me do a double-take. It asked, "What do you want to be when you grow up?" and as I re-read my own childish chicken-scratch several times, I laughed out loud to myself.

I had written that I wanted to be a "horse rider and an artist."

I know from my mother that I had maybe seen a horse *once* in person at that point in my life—my cousin Becky, who rode horses, had given me a pony ride. No one in my immediate family had any connection to horses. I didn't have friends who rode or a farm nearby where I might have gazed longingly at horses beyond a fence line. I think my main exposure to horses in my early life was the *My Little Pony* cartoon television show and the plastic toy versions of the show's horse characters that I played with.

So how was it possible that I knew I wanted my life to revolve around them? And that I would someday go to college to earn a degree in fine arts? And that love for both horses and art would hold true almost two decades later? Were these experiences I knew from prior lives that had left imprints on my very young heart? There was no logical explanation for my childish musings about my future to be as accurate as they seemed to be turning out to be.

I have learned over the course of my own life and through observing the lives of those around me that you can't take the love of horses out of a "horse person," nor can you "insert it" if it isn't already there. You either have such a love, or you don't. It seems to be something you're born with—something in your blood, in your DNA, woven into the fiber of your being. Denying it causes emotional distress and leaves one with the perpetual sense that something is missing in life...I've run that experiment on myself more than once, each time with the same result, leading me to the same conclusion: a life without horses just isn't possible for me. This is true for every horse person I know. Interestingly, it's almost impossible for a "non" horse person to understand, try as one might. There aren't many other experiences that compare. It's a passion and a compulsion, bordering on addiction.

We simply cannot help ourselves.

So those of us with this affliction look to find our place in the horse world. For some, it's a love that is fed in every minute of spare time, with a "real job" worked to fund the passion. For others, like me, your passion becomes your career.

This is a tricky path, because the lines between work and play, job and hobby, become blurred. *It is all-consuming.* You eat, sleep, and breathe horses. You dream about them. You worry about the financial feasibility of your life's pursuit, and its effect on those you love. You wonder If you're ever going to "make it" in the equine industry. You wonder what "making it" even means. Sometimes you contemplate quitting, even though, deep down, you know you can't ever stop completely. You recognize the insanity of your path while knowing there is no other path you would rather take in this life. You can see logically how silly it all is—the money, the worry, the time, the endless conjecture about your horse's health and happiness. But it also makes your heart sing and the beauty of it can move you to tears.

So for you, it's all worth it.

Sometimes *you just love what you love.* No rhyme or reason, no good explanation as to why. Even when your chosen path leads to heartache and headaches. Even when it leaves you subsisting on ramen noodles and peanut butter so your horse can have a chiropractic treatment and a shoeing upgrade. Even when every non-horse person in your life has no earthly idea what you do with your time or your money. Even when you recognize there could be an "easier" path out there.

Following a passionate path usually isn't easy, and sometimes you want to get off the ride, but most of the time, that love is enough. Love is what has kept me going, even when self-doubt consumed me and I had no idea where I was going. Every time I searched my heart, horses were there, filling it up and propelling me forward.

1
FINDING COMPASSION AND CURIOSITY

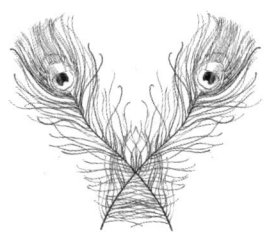

AS A STUDENT at Black Rock Elementary School in Thomaston, Connecticut, I was part of a Girl Scout troop that met weekly, either at a member's house or at the school. We learned general life and outdoor survival skills that earned us colorful badges to add to the brown sashes that completed the traditional Girl Scout uniform. Our troop became a primary friend group for many of us, and there were many sleepovers and birthday parties, and always cookies to sell (or consume).

When Connecticut Girl Scouts turned ten years old, we had the opportunity to attend a sleepaway summer camp called Camp Laurel. The members of my troop all eagerly awaited the year we could start going. Now being a parent myself, I can also see why the idea of a two-week sleepaway camp must have been thrilling for my single mother! When she approached me about Camp Laurel and pointed out I could choose to focus on horseback riding as an activity while there, of course I was in. I had *zero* fears about leaving home and spending time with people I had never met, in a place I had never been, because there would be *horses*.

At that point in my life, I had maybe laid my hands on an actual real live horse a couple of times total, but I was completely obsessed with the idea of riding and caring for them. I daydreamed about what it would be like to be on horseback every day while I watched my mom iron tiny patches with my name on them onto my clothes, and my pink towels and washcloths. Together we gathered all the toiletry items I was instructed to bring with me, and packed the clothes and boots that were unique to those campers in the riding program. On drop-off day, we drove for almost two hours to Camp Laurel, but I have no memory of anxiety or tears or fears of homesickness. What I do remember is being almost blind to the other campers and families around me as I said goodbye to my mom, focused solely on when I would get to be with the horses.

I think I always struggled a bit to fit in "normally" in social groups. I can recall, from a very young age, either being completely unaware of those around me or overly worried about how I was being perceived and if I was liked by my peers. Whenever I felt self-conscious and under the microscope of others' scrutiny, I avoided expressing an opinion and just agreed with the most prevalent one shared around me, so as not to set myself apart. I had a couple of close friends at school—students who were also in my Girl Scout troop—but I also sensed I was the subject of ridicule. I could tell I was being made fun of, but I didn't know for what.

Camp Laurel mirrored my social experience at school. I wished to be accepted by my peers and hoped desperately to make friends. I carefully observed the quickly forming cliques around me, decided which ones I wanted to be part of, then internally molded myself into the person I thought those kids would most want to hang out with—and be least likely to make fun of. The only time I didn't feel the impulse to conform to be like those around me was when I was with the horses. I was so enthralled with learning about them—about their daily needs and how to care for them, about the way they smelled and felt under my hands, about how they looked at me and interacted with each other—there was no room for insecurity. The horses' profound ability to exist in the present moment gave me the gift of that same experience. I had no words to express what I sensed in their company then, but looking back, I can still summon the feeling. The feeling I have around horses today is just as fresh and vivid.

From the first day of camp, I was drawn to Smokey, a big gray horse with a calm way about him that allayed any anxieties I may have felt about actually sitting on the back of a horse. Every day I waited with bated breath for the counselors to announce the horse that would be my mount for the morning and afternoon sessions. I would chant in my mind, *Please be Smokey...please be Smokey*. When our names were paired, I would say a little internal *Yessss!* and proceed to the barn with a skip in my step.

The few times it wasn't Smokey's name read out after mine, I was teamed with a small bay mare named Delilah. I knew nothing about horse behavior or reading horses at that point in my life, but hearing her name left me with an uneasy feeling. I had seen Delilah rear up on her back legs more than once when other campers or counselors worked with her, and I had watched several other people drop their stirrups, release their grip, and slide down her back over her haunches to land on the ground behind her when she did it. I was very nervous about the possibility of the mare rearing with me, but since the organizers kept giving campers Delilah to ride, I assumed her behavior was normal for a horse and I just needed to be prepared in case it happened. In my head, I replayed over and over what I had seen others do when she reared, mentally readying myself in case our names were called together.

The first time I was paired with Delilah, there weren't any major incidents, though in my mind, I was ready for whatever she might do. But even though she didn't rear, I didn't get the same feeling with her that I had when I rode Smokey—like he and I were on the same page, moving quietly in the same direction, relaxed and comfortable with each other. It was quite the opposite with Delilah. I got the sense she just wanted the riding to be over so she could go back to her turnout, away from people.

The second time I was given the bay mare was a day when all the campers were riding bareback. It wasn't very long into our lesson before she planted her feet and stood up on her hind legs. *I need to exit quickly, like I have been preparing to do*, I thought. I let go of the reins and slid down her back and onto the ground, landing squarely on my feet behind her. Delilah, for her part, landed back on all four legs and stood quietly. (Thank goodness she didn't kick out, as no one suggested I move away from her hind end.) The counselors had another rider get on her, who also ended up dismounting in a similar way when Delilah stood up. A third attempt was made by a different camper, but the rearing pattern continued. I now understand that Delilah had learned a behavior that met her needs. She wanted to be done working, and she'd found a way to make that happen. She was no dummy, that's for sure.

It was a daily roll of the dice for the camper who was paired with the little bay mare. Sometimes she would do the basic work without much complaint, but with an "edge" I perceived as her wanting to be done as soon as possible. Sometimes she would simply refuse to do *anything*, planting her feet immediately and rearing just enough to send the message that she was not interested in participating that day. This meant that every day of camp I internally begged whatever higher power might be in charge of such decisions that I would be paired with Smokey, and *not* with Delilah. I wasn't frightened of her, I just craved the experience of ease and flow that came with riding Smokey, rather than the feeling of being considered an annoyance that I got from Delilah. I longed for what all of us long for when we get on a horse: flow and freedom and a connection to something bigger than ourselves. I could feel that Delilah didn't open herself to the people around her. I could sense her disconnection from us, even though I could not describe or understand it at the time. I felt bad for her, but given I did not know any way to help her, I wanted to avoid her as much as possible.

With the knowledge I have now, I feel so much empathy for everyone involved with the horse program at Camp Laurel. The counselors were in their late teens and early twenties, so their life experience and horse experience was still very limited. On top of that, they didn't know the horses well, as a different batch of "camp horses" was brought in for use each summer. Organizers were given a large number of young, excited girls and a limited number of horses for them to work with. There was a math puzzle to be solved every day to make sure every rider was paired with a horse for each session. Some of those horses were happy, willing participants in the process, like Smokey. Others, like Delilah, were clearly not. Of course, now I wonder if Delilah was in some sort of physical pain that led her to react to being ridden in the ways that she did. Or perhaps her prior life experiences had taught her that shutting down mentally and refusing to engage with people when she felt overwhelmed or overworked led to an outcome she favored. What I know for certain is that both humans and horses were in an impossible situation at that camp.

What I experienced with Delilah at Camp Laurel is not a unique scenario in the horse world. We see it all the time: A person purchases a horse and before long, she runs into issues in the relationship she's trying to build with her new partner. She has no budget to purchase a different horse, and so feels the pressure to "make it work" with the one she has. She may not have the wherewithal to seek professional help in discerning what could be causing the unwanted behavior in the horse, or she may wish to seek help but not have access to the kind she and her horse need. So both horse and human go on, unhappy in each other's company, sometimes making very slow progress together, and sometimes simply bumping their heads into the same wall for years on end. In the worst cases, horse or human end up hurt, either physically or emotionally. Just like at Camp Laurel, people often don't know what they don't know, and horses can't help but live in the present and express how they feel in every moment.

I have discerned that, after being both the person who didn't know what she didn't know (and getting myself into sticky situations), and the person who helps those who find themselves in that difficult scenario, *compassion* and *curiosity* are key for everyone involved. It's easy to see what we believe to be a horse "suffering," to become angry about his perceived plight, and to blame the people we think are causing it. And, for sure, it is the responsibility of humans to do right by the animals we take into our care. I also believe, however, that *every one of us* has been in the position of learning new information, then looking back at all the places where we wish we could have applied it to the horses in our lives. We can see our mistakes so clearly in hindsight, and all the wishing and "should-ing" in the world won't change how we handled a situation *before* we "knew better." I try to be compassionate with *myself* around this subject, which is hard at times. I am not proud of the way I treated some of the past horses in my life, but at the time, I had no way of doing things differently. *I was doing the best I could with the information I had.* Most of the time, I think this is true of every person who loves horses, so I try to apply this understanding to others, as well as myself. I also try to look back at those situations with curiosity, asking myself what could have been going on with a particular horse and how could I have solved a problem differently. Oftentimes, being curious about the situations from my past has led to a better plan with the horses currently in my life.

For me, the importance of compassion holds even more true for the horses than the humans, as horses have no way to go and seek new information like we do. They can only draw on what they experience through what we ask of them. When a horse is behaving in a way we don't like, they most likely have learned that behavior through interactions with other humans. The horse has little reason to change behaviors that have "worked" for him in the past. Horses instinctually seek *safety* then *comfort*, and they learn how to get those basic needs met. When they feel their safety or comfort are threatened, they learn how to find those things again by any means necessary. That might be by bucking, or rearing, or trying to get back to the barn or their turnout, or yanking the reins out of someone's hands, or any number of so-called "bad" behaviors we see in horses.

Luckily for humans, horses are generally so forgiving that many will allow their safety and comfort to be impinged upon to a high degree, time and time again, before they try to change their situation. It is remarkable how much they allow us to do with them that goes against their natural instincts. How can anyone become angry at a horse for unwanted behaviors when we now know this is how horses operate? We aren't angry at babies when they cry to be fed, because that is what they have learned gets their needs met, and they have no other means to that end. Sure, it's natural that we get frustrated when things don't come as easily as we like or when we don't understand what is causing a behavior. *That's human*. For me, when I find myself frustrated in this way, the antidotes are always *compassion* and *curiosity*—for the self and for others.

For example, when I have a horse who clearly tries to avoid being bridled, I have a couple of choices: I can try to put that horse in a place where he cannot get away from me, hold onto him tightly, and wrestle the bit into his mouth and the bridle onto his head. Or I can take a moment to observe the behavior. When does the horse start to avoid the bridle? When he sees me pick it up? When I take his halter off? When I raise the bridle to his head or present the bit to his mouth? Each option might be telling me something different about the horse's objection. It might be telling me he is physically uncomfortable with the way the bit hits his teeth or the way the bridle goes over his ears. Or it might be telling me that the horse has an overall negative emotional relationship to the tacking-up process. I don't want to dance with an unwilling partner. I want my horse to accept the tack that allows us to communicate with each other, and that means willingly opening his mouth for the bit and standing quietly for the bridle to be set in place properly. So first I am *compassionate* about the expression of discomfort, be it physical or emotional, and then I am *curious* about how I can help mend it. I will likely have to slow down and break the process into small pieces for my horse. I will need to make a precise training plan and stick to that, no matter how slow the progress, in order to build a sense of trust and a clear line of communication.

In the end, it will be worth the time I take, because my partner will be a willing one.

2
FINDING EARLY TEACHERS
———

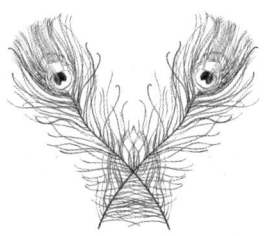

AFTER MY FIRST two-week equestrian adventure at Camp Laurel, my mom gave me a choice. I had been interested in learning to dance, but as a single-income household, financial realities meant I couldn't have both dance classes and riding lessons. I thought about the options for a brief moment, but horses were the clear winner. My mom, very much a *non*-horse person, then set out to find me a place to ride. This was before the days of online Google searches, so I actually have no idea how she connected with the owners of Pie Hill Equestrian Center in Goshen, Connecticut, but it ended up being a great place for me to start, because the local Pony Club was based out of that farm.

    As soon as I arrived at Pie Hill, I knew I had found my people. It was filled with other horse-smitten girls around my age, all dying to spend as much time as humanly possible at the barn. The farm owners, Penny and James, were happy to have the chaos and activity that came with a crowd of kids at their facility, I think in large part because we helped with the chores. Looking back, especially now as a professional and a farm owner myself, I can see how unhealthy their reliance on a young volunteer staff sometimes was for all involved, but at the time, for me, it was heaven. It also helped my mom because

Penny and James were willing to trade some lessons for my help at the farm after school and on weekends.

Pie Hill Equestrian Center was very different from the summer camp setup at Camp Laurel. It was a New England-style farm with a giant old house set on the top of a large rolling hill. It had a modestly sized wood-framed indoor arena that attached at one short end to a long, dirt-floored barn aisle, lined with stalls on both sides. Together, the barn and the indoor arena made the shape of a capital L. In the area between the long wall of the indoor and the length of the barn aisle, there was an open, outdoor riding arena with sand footing. A group of small paddocks with post-and-rail fencing hugged the end of the outdoor arena, and beyond them stretched a huge grass pasture where the majority of the horses were turned out together. A long chain served as the gate for the big field.

The property felt enormous to me that first day, as I had no riding facilities to compare it to, other than Camp Laurel. I immediately loved the smell of the place—a mixture of dirt, pine shavings, leather, and horse poop—a smell that my mom was not nearly as fond of, as it clung like glue to my boots and clothing from that day forward.

When I started taking lessons at Pie Hill, I didn't own "real" riding clothes. I wore blue stretchy stirrup pants paired with one of the two t-shirts I owned that had horses printed on them. Penny advised my mom invest in a pair of heeled boots that resembled paddock boots, which we bought from a regular shoe store, and I used a shared helmet from the farm. I was slightly embarrassed about my outfits in comparison to the other girls' proper riding gear, but no one treated me any differently because of my clothing—we were all too busy being horse girls. I wanted to spend every moment of my time outside of school at the barn. I longed to be with my new friends, who seemed to accept me in ways that the kids at school just didn't.

Early on in my weekly lessons, I overheard Penny telling my mom that I had a lot of natural "feel." At the time, I had no idea what that meant, but it sounded like a compliment, and so I was proud of it. Now, having seen and helped many young riders who I would describe in the same way, knowing that I was one of those kids that riding just seemed to come naturally to means even more. The fact that I was "all legs and arms" with a short torso contributed tremendously to my intuitive balance on a horse.

I joined the Litchfield Pony Club, which was based at Pie Hill and included all the other young riders at the farm, almost immediately. I can honestly say that my time in that Pony Club gave me the best foundation for a life working with horses that I could have asked for. The "unmounted" meetings—where we learned equine knowledge related to their daily care, conformation, diseases, and first aid—provided more solid basics than I would have learned in a Bachelor of Equine Science program. (Later, when I contemplated going to college for Equine Science, I looked into the curriculum at several universities that offered such programs and realized that I already knew and had been tested on the entire four years of information, thanks to Pony Club.) And in the riding department, I was fortunate to start my way up through the Pony Club rating system (D–A) with the saintly school horses of Pie Hill.

First, there was Doughboy. He was as his name indicated—a pudgy, stocky horse the color of bread with an Appaloosa pattern across his ample hind end. He was kind and slow and patient with everyone who rode him. He was a farm favorite because he was so simple and sweet. For a lesson barn, he was worth his weight in gold, as is any horse like him. I didn't ride him for long because he was reserved for the most beginner riders, and his dance card was often quite full with newer and younger students. Penny knew Doughboy would help riders gain confidence and find joy in being around horses. It was his gift to this world.

Then along came Brewster, my first "heart horse." I think he was at least twenty when he arrived at Pie Hill. A former fox hunter who had been in more than one accident in the field and in a trailer, his spine was clearly misaligned. You could feel his off-kilter vertebrae beneath the skin and muscle of his neck. He was tall and thin like me, built like a Thoroughbred, mostly a dark bay but with a small blanket of white hair and dark spots over his haunches. He was over at the knees, so he wobbled slightly when he stood still for too long. His heart was twice the size of any horse I had ever met.

Penny paired me with Brewster upon his arrival at Pie Hill, and he quickly became the only horse I rode. I trusted him implicitly, and apparently so did the farm owners, because I was allowed to ride him whenever and wherever I wanted, including outside managed lesson time and all over the fifty-plus-acre farm. In both high summer and mid-winter, when the snow was fresh and deep, my barn friends and I would ride our horses out to the far end of the big pasture behind the barn, and then turn and let them gallop back to the stable in a group. Never once did I worry that Brewster would be out of control or lose his footing. Riding him was my source of freedom. I felt proud and confident whenever I was on his back. The self-consciousness and insecurity related to interacting with peers outside the barn that I had always struggled with melted away when I was with him.

Brewster's sainthood was confirmed in our first summer together when I attempted to jump the middle bar of a split-rail fence one sunny afternoon, my friends cheering me on and the farm owners nowhere in sight. I picked up a canter inside one of the small, unused paddocks near the outdoor arena, and turned toward the section of fence where the top rail had fallen down sometime prior and not yet been replaced. I pointed Brewster in the general direction of my chosen obstacle, squeezed my legs around his sides, clucked my tongue, and prayed as I grabbed his mane and bent forward toward his neck.

Though Brewster cleared the fence successfully (with absolutely no help from me), his wobbly knees buckled on the landing side, and I toppled right over his head, somersaulting and landing on my back, looking up at him. Somehow, he stopped his feet in place, without stepping on me. He looked down, giving me a curious sniff, seeming to wonder how I had gotten there. He didn't try to flee the scene. He simply waited for me to get up, get back on, and then make a second attempt, which I executed in the same exact fashion. The only difference was that Brewster's knees held strong, and I stayed on as we cantered away.

God, I loved that horse.

At the time, I had some vague sense of how lucky I was to have Brewster in my life, though only in looking back can I see that he was the rarest of rare gems—quiet and calm, but ready and willing to play whatever foolish game I came up with, on the farm or off, any weather, any season, steady as can be. I wish every one of my students today could have a horse like Brewster to learn from.

I was sad when Brewster needed to retire, but I didn't begrudge him the rest he clearly deserved. He had done so much for me, and it was obvious that he needed to live out the rest of his days grazing and being loved from the ground. This meant Mr. Radar Jet was my next mount. I was *not* prepared.

Radar was a long-in-the-back Quarter Horse cross who had a propensity for bucking people off every so often. I guess Penny and James thought I could ride through it, because I became "his person." There was an awareness in the back of my mind that the adults seemed slightly on edge about what Radar might do while I was riding him, and I know now that I translated that possibility into some defensiveness in me. I never trusted him like I did Brewster. I always felt a tiny bit nervous riding him, especially when jumping.

Despite my wariness and the adults' concern, Radar and I continued up the Pony Club D levels together, and I even took him out to an eventing schooling trial with some of my barn friends. Somehow, I didn't get bucked off on the cross-country course, though I begged him the whole way around the course, "Please don't buck…please don't buck." Looking back, it seems to me that Radar actually hardly misbehaved at all when I rode him, at least not the way I know he did with other riders. Maybe it's because I weighed around ninety pounds soaking wet, or because I had some ability to keep the tension out of my body even when I was internally a bit anxious. It was Radar who began teaching me to make sure my body language reflected what I knew I was supposed to be doing, rather than simply responding to the urgings of self-preservation from my brain stem. This is, in fact, a skill that I have worked to hone my whole riding life, as it has helped me with many a sensitive horse.

Whatever the reason he chose to mostly behave with me, I am very grateful that Radar kept his feet on the ground. A bad riding accident at that formative point could have really impacted how my life with horses unfolded.

As a kid, I saw more than one crazy horse-related accident. One friend's pony spooked as we were hacking up a quiet road back to Pie Hill at the end of a nice long group trail ride. As the pony took off in a panic, my friend fell off and the shoelace of her paddock boot got caught on the little hook of her safety stirrup, and she was dragged up the asphalt road on her back. You can imagine the injury that was inflicted on both my friend's body and her mind. She was never the same rider after that day—always more timid and anxious—which makes complete sense, given the trauma she experienced. She dropped out of the Pony Club a few years after the incident, and we lost touch.

Another friend of mine grew up learning from a wonderful horse named Duffer. He was to my friend what Brewster was to me—the ultimate schoolmaster and the best friend a young girl could have. Duffer had a condition that caused him to choke on grain unless it was soaked completely into a soupy mess, and as he got older, his choking episodes became more frequent. One day, Duffer had an episode that he could not recover from, and he had to be humanely euthanized.

My friend was beyond devastated by the loss of Duffer. She mourned him for a long while before her love of horses outweighed her grief, and she and her family looked for another horse. But the new one was no Duffer, and he landed her in the dirt time and time again during their first few months together. My friend lost confidence and rode less as we moved into our middle teen years. I'd considered our love for horses equal when we first met, and I think, at that time, anyone would have guessed that we would have both grown up to have careers working with horses. In the end, only one of us did, and I believe my friend's experience losing Duffer and getting an extremely challenging new horse may have changed her life's path.

Sure, I hit the ground my fair share over the years, and there is something to be said for the innate resilience of any person who actually makes a career of riding and training horses. I also think, however, that I was very fortunate to never have been really hurt—physically or emotionally—as a young rider. I've learned a bit about brain development and neuroscience, and I can see how accidents and sudden losses in the formative years of adolescence can lead to strong unconscious reactions, including a fear of pain so great that it can override any joy derived from horseback riding. I am grateful that what I loved about horses remained intact through my most formative brain development years, and I have that wonderful string of school horses—the very best teachers—to thank for it.

After my first couple years at Pie Hill, Penny and James purchased a farm in Litchfield, Connecticut, and moved their Pie Hill business, renaming it Litchfield Hills Equestrian Center. The new facility was in a more populated and wealthy area, which I am sure was part of their business plan, but it needed a lot of improvments to bring it into working order. There was a half-finished indoor arena on the property, which was a top priority to complete because a New England winter was coming. There were several barns, many in disrepair, and the stalls along one side of the indoor were unfinished and prone to flooding when it rained. There were a few individual turnout paddocks, but as with their old facility, mostly the horses went out in a big herd in a large field. Unfortunately, it was situated in a way that made it difficult to provide a water source.

It was clear that Penny and James' funds were tight and hiring help was not an option. This meant that I received very little riding instruction at this point in my life, as Penny and James were working constantly on fixing up the facility, while I did a lot of the daily barn work to keep things running smoothly. Despite this, I had advanced enough that it became necessary to find me a mount with a bit more athletic ability than their herd of school horses had to offer.

Through Pony Club, we found Sailor, a small chestnut Thoroughbred gelding who had been standing in a muddy paddock for a long time, leading to a severe case of thrush in all four hooves. Sailor was "given" to me for a year as a free lease, and I worked diligently to clear up the condition in his feet so he would be sound enough to ride. Despite my youth and inexperience, I managed to bring him back fully, and he eventually allowed me to practice jumping more than any horse I had ridden up to that point. Sailor had clearly been out and about to shows and rallies in his lifetime, and he became a wonderful teacher at regional competitions and through my Pony Club C1 and C2 ratings. I was so proud seeing our picture together in a local newspaper when we won our division at the show jumping regional championships. Sadly, our budding partnership came to an end when the lease's terms concluded, and he went back to his owners.

Next came Gabby, a been-there-done-that Warmblood type with a young adult owner who didn't have much time to ride. She offered me a free lease, which my mom and I quickly accepted. Gabby was as kind as they come, and my mom really liked being around him, which was unusual for her (as a non-horse person), and it spoke volumes about his personality. Unfortunately, he had soundness issues, and our time together, while lovely, was short-lived.

Gator was pretty much the opposite of Gabby: a lanky gray Thoroughbred gelding who was more athletic, sensitive, and scopey than any horse I had previously ridden. He was well-built and handsome, and being allowed to ride him was the goal of many young girls at Litchfield Hills. There was a challenge in that honor, however. Gator wasn't dangerous, but he required more skill and tact than the "regular" lesson horses did. He was the fanciest horse I had ever ridden, and I was so proud to be deemed capable of working with him. He gave me a real taste of that feeling of flying over jumps at speed. Riding him over fences upped my adrenaline just enough to be exciting and make me want more, while also being safe.

It's funny...you might think that I would have strong memories of sadness around the fairly constant turnover of horses in my young life, but I don't. I wished that I had my own horse like most of my friends did, but I also knew that wasn't a possibility in my single-parent family. I was grateful when I was able to lease a horse who was only mine to ride, who I didn't have to share with other people, but I didn't shed tears when those leases had to end. It became an expected cycle: I'd ride one horse for a while, and then, when our abilities diverged, move on to another. I know now that having the opportunity to ride so many different types of horses at a young age was a huge advantage to my later riding career, and maybe some part of me knew there were hidden benefits to my situation. Or maybe I was just so happy to have horses in my life at all that this beggar was not about to become a chooser. Either way, I enjoyed the parade of equine teachers from whom I had a chance to learn, and the ability to "roll with the punches" as horses moved in and out of my life still serves me well as a professional.

Today, there is a lot of controversy in the horse world about the buying and selling of horses. There is a camp at one extreme that believes once you acquire a horse, you should keep him and care for him until the day he dies, no matter what. And there is a camp at the other end of the spectrum that believes horses are a monetary commodity to be bought and sold at will and as tools for personal and professional gain. Thankfully, there are many fair and responsible stances in between. I have experienced the heartbreak of having horses sold out from under me by their owners, as well as the frustration of teaching a student who is inappropriately matched with a horse, but refuses to sell the horse and look for another, usually safer mount. The truth is, being able to acknowledge when a horse isn't right for you (or when you aren't right for him) is part of the business of riding and training horses professionally, and the frequent coming and going of horses in my young life certainly helped me understand and learn to navigate the emotional component of that process—though sometimes with less grace than I would like.

3
FINDING RESILIENCE

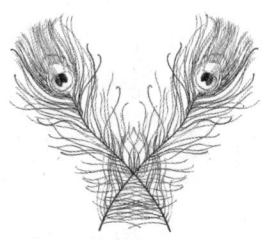

I TRULY WORKED MY TAIL OFF to keep horses in my life during the Pie Hill and Litchfield Hills years. I was often left solely responsible for the daily care of over twenty-five horses on weekends and during school breaks. This included mucking endless stalls that may or may not have been cleaned in the days prior to my shift. I pushed wheelbarrow after wheelbarrow of urine-soaked shavings and manure out of stalls that I knew should be kept cleaner for horses to live comfortably and in good health. I broke down, sobbing, on more than one occasion at the overwhelming amount of work still left to be done, feeling bound to my task by an overwhelming sense of responsibility for the animals who depended on me to care for them. Regular weekly lesson students and paying boarders would come and go from the farm all day, while I frantically tried to make sure the horses were fed breakfast before noon and all had clean water before their owners showed up and looked in their buckets. I wrestled with endless yards of leaky hose after turning the horses out, leading them in twos and threes, trying to make sure the farthest fields had full troughs, knowing they had probably not been filled the day before and that they may not be looked at for days to follow. I seldom, if ever, had help on my shifts.

There were times I showed up for scheduled lessons that I had paid for in hours and hours of manual labor, only to be tack-walking and waiting in the arena for thirty minutes before being told that my lesson was cancelled because Penny or James were busy with other things on the farm. Other times I wouldn't be told at all, and so I would just ride on my own, assuming I had been forgotten. I assumed this was the price I had to pay because we couldn't afford horses and lessons the way other families could. I thought what I went through was what barn girls everywhere endured. I believed the shorthandedness and dependence on my labor was just how lesson barns ran, because I didn't have anything to which to compare my experience. I also knew I couldn't live without horses, so I did what I had to do to keep them in my life. I never thought to tell my mother of my struggles, probably because I didn't want to risk her saying I could no longer spend time at the farm.

I muscled through those years, both physically and emotionally, loving and hating my little "horse world" at the same time.

There were other experiences during my years at Litchfield that were questionable—even dangerous. Like the time I was cleaning the stall of a two-year-old that grabbed me by the left knee with his teeth, pulled me off my feet, and dragged me halfway around his stall before letting go. No one had warned me of his aggressive behavior. His stall needed to be cleaned by someone, and though I was only thirteen at the time, I was the one on barn duty, so it fell to me. I didn't yet know how to read a horse's body language or have the tools and understanding to manage his behavior. Even though I went to Penny for medical care after the incident, there was no educational follow-up, explaining the why of what had happened or how it should have been handled. That horse could have killed me. Today, I cannot imagine ever allowing situations like that to occur on my own farm. A horse with aggressive behavior would be in a training program addressing the issue, and my staff would be coached in safe handling methods specific to his needs. If necessary, a horse I truly thought might be a danger to myself or others would be moved to another farm, as I am unwilling to put myself or my staff at risk for a monthly board check.

One day at Litchfield Hills, I went out to catch a horse from the group turnout field, and I noticed a liver chestnut Thoroughbred named Irving was dragging one front leg in a very strange way, hopping on his other three legs. As I got closer, I could see that Irving's leg was clearly broken below the knee as he feebly grazed, clearly in shock. I ran back to the barn to tell Penny—and that was literally the last I heard of Irving or the situation. I knew the veterinarian came and laid Irving to rest because I saw the truck come and go, but Penny and I didn't discuss what it had been like for me to find a horse in such a state. There was never a conversation about how such a tragic accident could be prevented in the future, nor was there a search of the field for holes or other possible causes. We didn't discuss how the news was or should be shared with boarders and other riding students at the farm. It is my feeling a child should never be expected to manage an experience like the one I had with Irving without support and guidance.

The incident with the aggressive two-year-old and Irving's death, as well as other more mundane experiences from my youth working at Litchfield Hills, clearly shaped the way I choose to run my own farm now. My priority is *safety*, first of human and then of horse.

Right on the heels of safety are *education* and *communication*. When problems arise that put people or horses at risk, I know that someone needs information, skills, and an understanding they may not already have. And unless I, my staff, or my boarders know there is a problem, a solution can never be reached. So clear, honest, and timely communication is an absolute must.

I have been at many barns where information is not shared between those working at the facility, which leads to the mishandling of horses. I have also been at many barns where gossip is allowed to run rampant among staff and boarders, leading to unnecessary drama and upset, which in my experience creates an environment that is uncomfortable and ultimately unsafe for everyone. Thankfully, I have learned a lot from the mistakes of others, as well as my own, over the past three decades. This has allowed me to cultivate the kind of farm community that I didn't even know existed when I started riding.

Between the ages of eleven and fifteen, I began to understand that two opposite things can be true at the same time. I learned that you can be the recipient of a huge amount of opportunity and good fortune, while also being put in impossible situations in order to hang onto them. Over time I have realized that, as people develop, it's up to them to decide the relative value of things in their lives. For example, how much suffering is worth the benefits received? We each have to learn our threshold of tolerance for the situations we end up in and the ways we allow ourselves to be treated. Unfortunately, we often don't learn that threshold until we have left a situation or are being treated differently, and thus have a means of comparison. At least then we "know better," so we can make better choices for our own well-being. Learning our innate value is an important life lesson that often comes from being undervalued. Then the question becomes, what do we do if we end up in that position again? Do we tolerate it by choice, believing that the benefits outweigh the difficulties? Do we decide to extricate ourselves, knowing that nothing is worth what we are enduring? Or do we not even realize that we are back in that position again until something big shakes us awake?

While I can say I will never knowingly put a young person in the positions I was put in during my teen years, I will also acknowledge that there was an aspect of character building to what I went through, and thankfully, I was resilient enough that the negative experiences didn't deter me from my passion. I also believe the benefit of having access to so many horses was worth the struggle. But it doesn't have to be that way. I believe that people can learn about horses and riding in emotionally and physically healthy environments, and still build strong moral character.

Each of us has the option to be grateful for what less-than-ideal experiences teach us, and to know how and when to move on, without burning bridges. This too is a skill worth learning, as the horse world is shockingly small.

4
FINDING THE INTANGIBLE

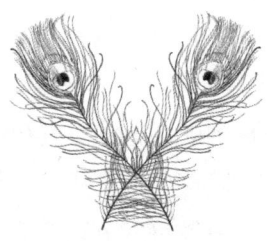

THANKFULLY, PONY CLUB eventually opened another door for me, leading me to Lost Run Farm, the home of Virginia Leary. Virginia had been an upper-level event rider, along with her husband Jack, and she coached some of the more advanced riders in our club. I was able to fairly trade my time and energy working at Virginia's farm for the opportunity to lease and receive lessons on a wonderful horse—a Connemara-Thoroughbred cross called Euglena. He was a bay gelding with a long back, a soft eye, a little white star on his broad forehead, and the kindest of hearts. Given how little I understood of how the process of training an animal actually worked at that point in my riding career, it was amazing how much "U.G." offered me during our time together. He carried himself on the bit, mostly forward and swinging his back, moving easily between gaits and smoothly laterally when I asked in any sort-of correct way. When coaxed gently, he would jump the beginner novice- and novice-sized fences I pointed him at, even though he was clearly tentative and a bit nervous. He was what I would now call a low-level schoolmaster, and I can honestly say he was the most forgiving creature I have ever met on this earth. He dealt with my teenage angst like a kindly teacher—calmly listening, and never interrupting or offering unsolicited advice.

I still carry guilt for the rides in which my frustrations with my non-horse life came out as anger at Euglena. There was one afternoon after school, in particular, when I arrived at Lost Run in a terrible mood, surely because of some boy-related issue. I brushed U.G. and tacked him up mindlessly, looking only to check our ride off my to-do list so that I could get back to attending to the teenage drama of the day. Not surprisingly, U.G. did not offer me his usual ease and suppleness, and I remember trying to "put" him on the bit by aggressively moving it back and forth in his mouth while crying my eyes out and pleading out loud, "Why won't you just go round?!" For sure he was not forward, nor was I asking him to use his body properly with any semblance of clarity. I was an emotional mess who had *no business* riding a horse that day. I was being unfair with U.G., but even then, he never put a foot out of place or complained. He still tried his little heart out for me, doing the best he could to interpret the frantic, stressed out, aggressive input I was giving him. Eventually, I called it quits for the day, the guilt over how I had treated U.G. already seeping in.

Partly due to his saintly attitude, Euglena and I made our way to Pony Club Nationals for dressage in Lexington, Virginia, as representatives of the New York/Upper Connecticut Region, and earned national placings in both team competition and our individual freestyle. He also helped me earn my B Pony Club rating, which was quite a feat for a horse that didn't really event, as it was equivalent to the United States Eventing Association (USEA) Training Level. He was not a brave horse, and we sometimes had stops on cross-country, but I was always able to get him to try and jump for me in the end.

Leaving Euglena to go to college was among the most painful things I had to do in my young life. He felt like home to me in a way that nothing else did. He was the first horse I really shed tears over—multiple times. First, when I was away at school, missing him dearly; then, when I found out he had been moved to his owner's home and I would no longer see him at Virginia's farm when I was home on break; and finally, when I learned he had colicked badly and had to be euthanized. Many of those final tears were shed in recognition of the fact that I hadn't truly appreciated what a gift he was to me. He had given me so much kindness and tried so hard for me, and I felt I had taken that for granted, never giving him nearly as much in return.

Later in my life, through meditation and the practice of self-compassion, I let much of the guilt related to U.G. go, and now I can look back on my time with him with love and gratitude. A picture of his sweet face at Pony Club Nationals lives on a dresser in my bedroom, and I can't help but smile every time I look at his soft eyes in that picture, feeling my heart fill up with love for him and the time we had together.

I have observed that horses have a capacity to help people become grounded in a way that other humans simply can't. That's what U.G. did for me. I think it comes from horses' ability to live so completely in the present moment, and to embody the qualities that many people see as the peak of goodness. They don't ask for more than they need, and they don't wield their strength and power to get anything but their needs met—even though they could. They are open to experiences as they come to them, and they seek the path of least resistance, never being malicious just for fun. Horses provide a space for humans to exist in all our turmoil and confusion, without judgment. They are therapeutic without exerting any effort to be so. No wonder we have been drawn to them for centuries.

I have often joked with fellow horse people that loving horses is like an addiction. Some of us can't live without them, and we are willing to arrange our lives so that we don't have to. As addictions go, horses are a mostly healthy, albeit expensive, coping mechanism for the trials and tribulations of life. To me, relying on another living creature to provide emotional stability in any way means we have a responsibility to understand that being's needs and meet them as best we possibly can. That also means we can never assume we know all the answers. It means we have a duty to continually educate ourselves in regards to how we care for and communicate with our equine charges. It means we must be perpetual students of those who study horses in different ways, and of horses themselves. We must be open to what horses have to teach us about themselves…and about *our*selves.

I have come to recognize what horses provide as similar to a profound experience I had one afternoon during my senior year of high school. I arrived at Lost Run Farm to do my usual chores, but when I walked into the barn, I was immediately sure that something was completely different about the space. I stood in the middle of the aisle, looking around at the familiar surroundings, alone and utterly confused, because, for the life of me, I couldn't put my finger on what had changed. I opened every stall door, and looked in the feed room, the tack room, the bathroom, the hay stall, then went back out the door and studied every side of the barn from every angle, but could not see a single thing that seemed out of place, anywhere. With more than a little hesitation and befuddlement, I started my afternoon chores, keeping a wary eye on my surroundings as I went.

Virginia arrived shortly after, and I immediately told her I had the feeling that something had changed, but that I could find nothing different at the farm. Virginia grinned and literally laughed out loud. She went on to tell me that she'd had the barn "cleared" that morning, explaining how her friend had come and done a "sage-burning ritual." I was stunned that something completely invisible to the eye had had such a palpable effect on a space I knew like the back of my hand. How was that possible? How could somebody waving around a bundle of burning herbs leave me with the sense that the space was completely transformed?

I think Virginia may have been as surprised as I was by my reaction that afternoon. Not long after, she invited me to sit with her and a group of other women, including her sage-burner friend, in a space on the Litchfield Town Green. We gathered on a circle of cushions and the other women took turns talking about their lives. I felt nervous, knowing that we would eventually come to me. I found myself shaking and crying uncontrollably as I began to speak, describing a feeling I sometimes had while lying in bed at night. It was a sensation of being larger on the inside than my skin would allow, a feeling that was so uncomfortable it would leave me both frightened and angry with no means of relief other than to will myself to sleep out of sheer emotional exhaustion.

I have no idea why I shared my nighttime suffering with the group of unknown women, sitting together that day, and I don't remember the exact advice they gave me, but I do remember they validated my feelings somehow, without trying to fix them, and allowed me to move through my emotions without pressure to change. From then on, whenever I would feel that frightening sensation, lying in my bed at night, it held far less power over me. Eventually it stopped happening altogether, I think because I stopped fighting it so hard. I robbed the fear of its power over me by allowing it to come and to go. The women who listened to me that day gave me permission to do that, simply by bearing witness to my story.

Horses offer us this same kindness. They bear witness to the stories we bring to them, without judgment and without trying to fix us. Euglena did that for me, over and over again, when I was a teenager. Horses are sage-burners, creating palpable shifts in the energetic world around them without leaving a trace.

I have learned there are times you can't clearly see a thing, but you can *feel* it. To me, feeling something experientially is just as real as anything you can see. I think this is an understanding held by people of strong religious faith, whatever their belief system might be. That being said, I didn't grow up following a particular religious path. I grew up surrounded by science and math teachers, to whom evidence was king. So, at first, the idea that something could exist without visual proof seemed like a contradiction. But how can I deny what I feel and know of the world through my experiences? If I do, it means I can't trust my own interpretations of those experiences. It means I have to deny what my heart, mind, and gut tell me, and instead trust only what others indicate is true.

I think horses help us bridge the gap between what we see externally, and what we sense and know innately, because they spend so much of their lives in a state of open awareness. Humans have access to a similar, natural state of being, but we override it with our thinking, moving minds. For example, there have been many times I have had a "gut feeling" that a horse just isn't feeling quite right. It is subtle—maybe just a slightly different swish of the tail, a more blasé attitude toward breakfast, or a slightly higher alertness in their posture. I may carry on with the horse's usual work for a few days, taking note of my initial suspicions and sensing if there are more or continued disturbances in his normal behaviors. If there are, and I decide to dig deeper, I almost always find something: the beginning of stomach ulcers; a tick-borne illness, like Lyme disease or anaplasmosis; a vitamin deficiency or a change in blood sugar levels;

or soreness somewhere in the body. When we practice existing in a state of elevated awareness, the way horses do, we become more conscious of subtle changes and quieter modes of communication. We learn to trust our instincts and listen more carefully. We start to catch little things before they become big problems.

This ability can bleed out beyond the barn, and we can learn to more aware in other areas of our lives. We can sense what's below the surface, not by weaving a story in our minds about what we *think* is happening, but by being open and allowing experience to occur. This is not only how we become better students and learners, but how we become better partners, parents, and educators.

5
FINDING LOVE OF LEARNING

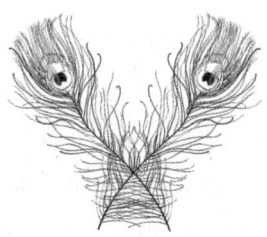

DURING MY HIGH SCHOOL YEARS, riding with the Litchfield Pony Club, I had the opportunity to work with trainers Steve Milne and Jenna Reveal, who had newly relocated from California to Connecticut and were leasing space at a privately owned facility called Thunder Ridge. Steve had been connected to Pony Club on the West Coast and so naturally reestablished that connection when he and his partner came east.*

From my very first lesson with Steve, the way he taught drew me in and engaged me in a way that was different than other instructors I'd had. He didn't just *tell* me what to do at every given moment. He explained the "why" behind what he wanted a rider to do, he gave the history of that "why," and then he mused about how the "why" might evolve over time as we learned more about horses. He quoted horse people I had not yet heard of, and he clearly had a thirst for learning that outweighed the desire to be right. He was a "horse nerd" in the best sense of the word.

It turns out it takes one to know one.

For the first time, I began to understand a bit about how horses

---

*I should note here that in 2020 Steve was banned from participating in any activities and competitions that USEF licenses, endorses, or sponsors, due to Safe Sport Sanctions. I never, in my time working with Steve, personally experienced or witnessed anything that made me uncomfortable or felt inappropriate.

think and process information. With Steve's encouragement, I started to wonder how to *actually teach* a horse things, rather than just ride him. Steve introduced me properly to the concept of pressure and release in its purest form, with the goal to always use the lightest aid possible, only add pressure as necessary, and always return to a neutral place of connection when a horse even *tried* to find the answer. With this guidance, I started to mature from having a natural "feel" for riding to *actually* feeling horses respond to the questions I was asking them. I realized there was a two-way conversation in a new language happening between us, and that with careful attention, I could gently guide it.

For the first time in my years of working with and around horses, I began to learn the importance of a mutually respectful relationship on the ground as well as when on the horse's back. I learned how to ask a horse to walk quietly with me from Point A to Point B, and how to teach that horse about my personal space when he didn't understand how to stay out of it. I began to understand that every moment I was in visual range of a horse, I was teaching him something, and I might as well make that something useful. I learned how to "bring up" my energy to get something accomplished beside or on a horse, and how to "bring down" my energy afterward and move on quietly, all without involving my emotions. I was taught the Classical Training Scale for flatwork (rhythm, suppleness, contact, impulsion, straightness, collection) and Steve's training scale for jumping (line, pace, distance, balance, impulsion) and how the time I took building clear communication about these elements on the ground would positively influence my riding. I started to comprehend how every horse had something to teach me about honing my communication skills and gladly offered to "catch-ride" anything and everything I was invited to sit on, from the opinionated 13-hand pony to the very young and green Friesian sent to my local barn for short-term training.

Steve never sugarcoated things for me or tried to inflate my ego. In fact, he reminded me—often—that ego had no place in training horses. When other people praised me and told me I was talented and "going places," Steve would simply continue to instruct me. He didn't placate me, but there was never any meanness either. He was never unfairly tough. He always repaid the time I put in working at his farm with lessons and thanked me for my hard work, while holding me to a high standard of care for the horses. While he joked a lot, he was amiable even when he was serious, and he had clear expectations of both the humans and horses in his life. I felt I knew where I stood with him, which is something I realized later on that horses *also* appreciated. Clear, kind, and consistent expectations make for an excellent learning environment.

I assume Steve knew that he was a bit of a father figure for me. The importance of that positive and stable male role model in my life during my tumultuous teen years is something that I wouldn't understand until much later, but looking back on it, I am so incredibly grateful for the time he gave me and the lessons I learned from him. It's funny—the relative time I spent with Steve before I headed off to college was short in comparison to the time I'd spent with other instructors through the years. Somehow, though, it felt like I'd worked with him for longer than anyone else. I think this is because it was with Steve that the "lightbulb" turned on for me. It was under his guidance that I started to see horses and my relationship with them differently, and it was at that time that I also began to think more deeply about their importance in my life. Now, looking back, I feel so fortunate to have had that opportunity relatively early in my riding career, because what I learned with Steve shaped its entirety.

There are so many "core horsemanship understandings" Steve taught me that are still integral to my current work, it's hard to list them, but in these pages, I'd like to give it a shot:

- Firstly, he taught me *there is always more to learn and no one knows it all.* This understanding is a character trait I admire in the instructors I seek out in the world, to this day, and it's one I try to embody for my own students. It translates into a willingness to learn from every experience we have, even the tough ones. It is displayed in a genuine humility that is balanced by healthy self-confidence. That combination is magnetic to me, and when I am drawn to someone as a teacher, those are usually the primary ingredients in the individual's personality. Though having an ego is undoubtedly a part of being human, I naturally seek those who can manage whether their ego has control over their ability to be open with others and to new ideas. I have found the trainers who are aware of this balance are among the most curious and compassionate people in the world, embodying two of the characteristics I value most in training and in other people.

- Steve constantly reminded me to *slow down.* "The hurrier you go, the behinder you get" was one of his favorite sayings. I learned the lesson held in this phrase the hard way, time and time again. Whether you are an adolescent with boundless energy or a "type A" adult, there never seems to be enough time to do all the things that need to be done on a farm full of horses. Add in horse-showing and non-farm responsibilities, and even as a teenager, I was often left with a sense of panic about time that led to hurrying through tasks. Inevitably this would lead to a mistake that would take even more time to correct. When I was young, Steve's attitude sometimes came across as lackadaisical, but I now see that he was simply taking his time so that he wouldn't have to go back and fix the mistakes he would have made if he had hurried. Whenever I find myself feeling like I don't have enough time to get everything done, I try to take a breath and go about my tasks methodically, without rushing. This hasn't always been easy, especially as my life has become more and more full. But when I can manage it, I know slowing down pays off.

Despite his "slow down" philosophy, Steve also taught me what it means to hustle: "I'll sleep when I'm dead" was another of his favorite sayings. Many times, I saw him exhausted to a point no human can usually withstand for any length of time...except maybe parents of newborns. I knew he kept going because there were things that simply needed to be done, and he refused to do a half-assed job. Looking back, I don't believe these were always the healthiest choices, but Steve always pressed on, knowing there would be an opportunity to slow down when needs were met and to-do lists were shorter. When the target shifted or got farther away, Steve would dig deeper, somehow without burning out. Throughout my life, I have tried to emulate his tenacious drive toward a chosen end point. I try to prioritize, set goals, and *work*, as methodically as I can. Often, I don't stop with what absolutely *has* to be done, and push into what I *want* to get done before I call it a day. That line between "has to" and "want to" can be very blurry, and I have found that being willing to step over it sets a person apart from others in their field. That is what it means to hustle.

Steve showed me *there is joy in seeing someone you help succeed*. It's easy to get wrapped up in one's own goals, even if you train others in your area of expertise. But I have been surprised more than once by the delight I feel when someone I have been helping has a breakthrough moment or surmounts a personal challenge. It doesn't matter if it's an accomplishment at a big "rated show" or a small step in the right direction on the ground in the home arena—the pride I could see in Steve when he had this kind of experience, and that I have become familiar with in my own life, is sometimes bigger than what is triggered by one's own accomplishments. In this way, we can reach out beyond ourselves and positively affect the lives of others. It feels fruitful, like time well spent, and hard work paying off in a way that can be celebrated together. It's a beautiful thing to measure one's own success by the success of those you help.

It was Steve who showed me that *knowledge trumps guts*. He was the first to admit that he was not an overly brave person; you might be surprised to learn I would consider myself quite similar. He taught me that having a toolbox full of tools helps lower anxiety, because you can rely on the fact that you have what you need to get the job done. We all have a survival instinct that kicks in well before our prefrontal cortex takes over with rational thought. We can't help it. It's part of how we evolved, and it's what keeps us safe and alive, most of the time. The trick becomes noticing when the "flight, fight, or freeze" response has taken control of the ship unnecessarily, and then looking at *what we know* for answers instead. Life, for me, is *an inexhaustible search for knowledge*. I don't just want a little plastic handheld toolbox—I want one of those *giant* ones on wheels, with more drawers than you can count. I want it to hold so many tools that I forget what is in the back of the bottom right drawer until I go digging. With a knowledge toolbox like that, I don't have to rely on the bravery I wasn't naturally born with. I can use my uniquely human brain instead. Sure, it's helpful to have brains *and* guts, but if I had to choose just one of the two, it would be brains, every time.

I also learned that when you trust your trainer, you might find out you are actually better than you think you are. I learned this lesson most distinctly one summer afternoon in my late teens when Steve asked me to jump a very small pony over what seemed, at the time, like a very tall jump. I was long-legged enough that I had felt the bottom of my boots, which hung below the pony's belly, brush the top rail the first time we went over. I didn't think the pony (or I) could do it a second time, so I hemmed and hawed when Steve told me to come to it again. He gave me one more chance to comply with his request, but I was too scared. Without preamble, Steve told me to leave the ring, which I did, in tears. He didn't yell at or scold me. He simply said that if I was unwilling to be taught, then the lesson was over, and I could leave. In that simple demonstration, he showed me that he believed in me in a way I didn't believe in myself. By not getting angry about my decision to leave rather than try the jump again, he left me with the understanding that he was there to help me when I was ready to believe in myself as much as he did. I have used similarly clear tactics with more than one of my own students over the years, and it enhanced my relationship with those students, rather than damage it.

Finally, Steve taught me the practice of *paying it forward*. Even when I was young, I always knew that Steve did a lot for me that he wasn't paid to do. He brought me to countless shows, gave me constant instruction both in and out of the saddle, took time to teach me how to drive a truck and trailer (which my mother was terrified to do), and always made room for technical and philosophical discussions about horse management, training, and riding, whichever of us instigated it. I believe I received so much more than I gave in money, time, and labor. So when I see others who maybe don't have "the means" but who are willing to work their asses off, I am very much inclined to help them. I see myself in them, the way I'm sure Steve saw himself in me. Without his willingness to give me that early metaphorical *leg up*, I would not be where I am today. I can only hope that someone in the horse world will hold me in the same high regard someday.

6
FINDING HUMILITY

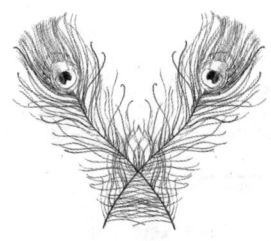

MY MOM DIDN'T give me a choice about going to college. All I wanted to do when I graduated high school was work with horses, full time, but she was adamant that having a degree to fall back on was important. I don't necessarily agree with that point of view even now, especially as higher education costs continue to skyrocket disproportionately, compared to the salaries that college graduates usually earn. But I do think there's a lot of "growing up" that happens in the years after high school, when the human brain is still maturing, and jumping into a career at that moment may not be the right answer either. No one is ready to make long-term life decisions when the brain is still years away from a fully functioning prefrontal cortex. For me, college ended up encouraging me to explore aspects of myself outside the horse world, which was just as important to my development as a human and a horseman.

Of course my mom preferred I get a "useful" degree of some sort, but as I've already mentioned, all the equine studies programs I considered seemed redundant after my years in Pony Club, and the only thing I "loved" at the time, besides horses, was art. So I decided to pursue a degree in fine arts, and after visiting a few schools in New England, the University of Connecticut offered me both in-state tuition and great scholarships. Plus, they had a school-run horse farm right on campus that I could walk to from my dorm. Granted, it was a Morgan Horse breeding program, which was outside of my wheelhouse at the time, but it meant I could ride and be around horses, which I knew was an absolute necessity if I was going to make it through the next four years.

Interestingly enough, the friends I made in my first year of college were not horse people, though the barn did continue to be a respite for me from the social and educational pressures of university life. The farm managers noticed my ease around the horses and my riding ability, and offered me opportunities to work with the horses outside of standard student lessons. I always felt more at home in my own skin at the barn than I did anywhere else on campus, even the art studios. There was still an aspect of trying to "fit in" in other spaces that just wasn't as present when I was around horses. I knew who I was with horses, and I didn't feel like I had to create a persona to blend in at the barn.

One evening, during my first semester at school, the barn brought in a guest speaker—a woman named Beth Baumert, who I learned was a long-time professional dressage trainer based nearby. During her talk, she asked the audience a few questions about the basics of dressage, like, "Does anyone know what the first step in the classical dressage Training Scale is?" No one raised their hand to answer her questions—except me. Beth noticed, and at the end of her lecture, she invited me to visit her farm, noting she was looking for a bit of part-time help and was happy to exchange lessons for manual labor, which was a trade I was well familiar with. I saw an opportunity to ride more horses and get good instruction; little did I know that Beth was very well known in the dressage world, and that, at the time, her daughter Jennifer was a rising star.

My first lesson with Beth was a very big reality check. Up until then I had been a big fish in my little Pony Club pond. I had taken riding more seriously than my peers at home and had been the only one who seemed to be planning on horses as the basis of a career. But I quickly gathered from Beth's reactions during our first session together that I was not quite the caliber of rider my knowledgeable answers to her lecture questions had led her to expect. I was not as polished or coordinated a student as she was accustomed to, and instructor compliments were not nearly as forthcoming as I was used to. That lesson left me questioning my skill set and ability, though I tried my best to see it and the following months as a valuable learning opportunity. I was fortunate in my time at Beth's farm to ride some very lovely horses and to work in an extremely well-run facility, but it was a very humbling experience. It was my first glimpse into the world of upper-level dressage, where horses were imported from Europe as a matter of course, and where there was a very specific track riders had to follow in order to be seen by the right people to advance their career.

I am so glad I was confident enough to speak up and answer Beth's questions during that evening talk all those years ago. My actions opened a door I didn't even know existed. Had I been too timid to raise my hand, I wouldn't have had the opportunity to ride at Beth's farm and learn from her. I would not have been humbled by her instruction, which was something I can now see I needed at that point in my riding career. It turned out to be quite a mild humbling in comparison to what awaited me in the years to come.

As part of moving up the levels in Pony Club, riders are expected to verbalize their equestrian experiences out loud, to reflect on what is going well and what could be improved in any given moment, and to verbalize a plan to move in that direction during the rest of each ride. This is also something that Beth, and every other instructor I have learned anything valuable from, has asked me to do during lessons. It is a skill learned only through practice and is not a comfortable process for most at the outset. But it is a practice worth making habit, as it breeds confidence over time and encourages a willingness to put oneself out there for feedback. You learn that it isn't always about being right as much as it is about inviting different perspectives or ideas about how to proceed toward the desired outcome. Verbalizing experiences out loud during riding lessons enables you to do so elsewhere in your life and take those risks that might just pay off in ways you don't expect.

I ask my students to tell me about their intentions for themselves and their horses at the outset of their lessons, and to describe what they are feeling in themselves and from their horses during their rides. I try to reflect what they say back to them, so they can make adjustments to their descriptions and expand their horsemanship vocabularies. Many students find this hard to do at first, especially when much of the equine vernacular is still foreign to them. I know they would prefer it if I simply told them what I am seeing and what they should do moment to moment, but if I took that route, I would be depriving them of an opportunity to become more present in their work and in our interactions, which, as we know, is also a skill worth honing. Today, my goal in helping people with their horses is to create independent thinkers who understand that they are training their horses in every moment they are interacting with them. I want them to take that responsibility seriously, and to think critically about the training process and their role in it. I want them to be curious about the "whys" as much as the "hows" of training, and I absolutely love it when students come to lessons with an idea or a theory that is new to me.

My favorite students are those who diligently try to improve each time I see them. I honestly don't care if a person is a beginner rider learning how to walk and trot, or an upper-level rider trying to perfect a difficult movement or smooth out a jumping round. When a student is making mistakes in every session because she is trying to do things differently enough to improve, then I am thrilled. I don't care if she progresses at a snail's pace, as long as I see the student *trying*...and running the experiment of, *"What will happen if...?"*

The most difficult students to teach are those who come to their lessons every week and pay me to tell them the same exact thing I told them the week prior. For sure, it's up to each rider to establish personal goals for growth, if growth is indeed desired. I can't make others work harder or push them outside their comfort zones unless they are willing participants, but it's hard for me to understand riding apathy. Even when you don't have Olympic aspirations or the goal to compete at any level, aren't you interested in communicating with your horse more clearly? In understanding what your horse is telling you in your time together? Isn't there always something in your horsemanship that you can learn and improve upon?

I get the sense from people who get stuck in a repetitive lesson cycle that there may be fear behind their stagnation. Maybe it's a fear that their horse will do something unpredictable or frightening if they try something new. Or maybe it's a fear of looking silly or seeming like they don't have all the answers. Whatever the reason, I encourage a bit of self-examination on this point. I can't name a single positive change in my life, or in the lives of people close to me, that has come without a bit of difficulty. I can't remember ever learning something new that made a positive impact on my life that didn't contain an aspect of being uncomfortable as I tried to grasp it.

I encourage my students to practice leaning into discomfort, even when it's not something they choose to do every day…even if it's just an experiment, once in a while. After all, they are already game to sit on a thousand-pound animal and ask it to do their bidding. There must be some part of them that enjoys a challenge and a little bit of risk.

When resistance to trying something new pops up, I suggest students become curious about the fear that might be behind it. I encourage them to listen to the fear, as if a good friend was explaining a worry to them. I remind them that they are not one and the same as their fear. They can be present with it, listen, feel, allow it to pass, and then get practical about it: What skills could they learn that would allow them to execute a plan beyond their fear? I try to help them break things down into small steps, the way we would for a horse that is anxious or doesn't understand, and I remind them that just outside of their comfort zone is *exactly* where learning and improvement happens.

7
FINDING A WAY THROUGH SHAME

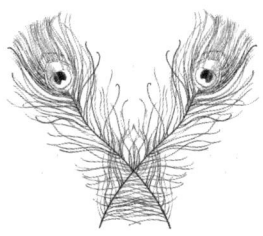

NEAR THE END of my freshman year at the University of Connecticut, I began looking for a horse that I could ride for my Pony Club A-level ridden test. The United States Pony Club has established Standards of Proficiency that provide riders a clear progression of skills from Level D (beginner) through A (advanced), and in order to receive a particular rating, you have to demonstrate your knowledge and ability in front of USPC examiners. I had ridden lesson or lease horses through all my other ratings (or certifications), but at the time I didn't have access to a mount that had the physical capabilities necessary for the A-level eventing test, which was about equivalent to running Preliminary level at a USEA-rated event. Pony Club hadn't yet separated out the different discipline paths you could follow to reach your A rating, like it offers now (dressage, eventing, show jumping, hunter seat equitation, Western dressage, and Western). It was one track—eventing—and I had one more summer before I was going to age out of Pony Club youth member status when I turned eighteen. It was important to me to attain my A rating before then.

I found an ad in a local newspaper for a horse for sale that sounded like a potential option: a Thoroughbred gelding that apparently had a good bit of jumping experience and had been sitting idle since his owner had gone off to college a year or two prior. His owner's parents wanted to find the horse a new home, as he was living by himself in their backyard, costing them time and money. I arranged to drive to their nearby location and meet him.

When I arrived, I was introduced to Mikey, a very large-boned, seventeen-hand chestnut with a kind, relaxed eye and a willing manner. I only rode him on the flat, as his small paddock was also the riding space, and he was so out of shape I didn't dare jump anything. I also didn't have the money to purchase him, even for the few thousand dollars the family was asking (in today's market, a horse like Mikey would likely go for around twenty-five thousand). But his owner's parents were willing to work out a deal: We agreed I would take the gelding for the summer, get him back in shape, show him, use him for my A rating, and then help sell him, giving the family the profit. I saw it as a win-win for everybody, and thankfully so did they.

Little did I know what a huge undertaking I was embarking on and what a giant "ask" I would have been making of any horse. I cannot *imagine* taking that kind of leap now. Looking back, I have such a deep appreciation for Mikey, as he was clearly an incredibly generous being. Just the fact that he was living alone, fairly content in that backyard, seems incredible to me now, not to mention the fact that he was so relaxed about some stranger showing up and riding him for what was the first time in years. I had lucked out again and didn't even know it.

When I shared my plan with Steve, he was (thankfully) willing to help. I think he was probably as doubtful about the situation as I would be if presented with it now, but as I've explained, he was always up for a challenge! Basically, I had four months to recondition Mikey, pass my A-level test, and get him sold. Because he was such a relaxed and willing horse, Mikey was game to try too. He was relatively straightforward on the flat, just lacking muscle and fitness, and as it turned out, he had a bigger jump in him than Steve and I ever could have guessed by looking at him. As he got in shape, the jumping got easier and easier. I have a picture of me jumping him over a huge oxer at the end of that summer, the rails at almost the top of a five-foot set of standards, and him clearing it with room to spare. I had never had a horse who was so simple to jump, and it was empowering!

Unfortunately, it also turned out Mikey had little-to-no dressage show or cross-country experience. I took him to a regional dressage rally and never made it more than three-quarters of the way down the centerline toward the judge's booth because he was so scared of it. We completed our test in the top three-quarters of the ring, our circles accurately shaped, though not in the proper locations. And it took Steve, Jenna, and I over an hour to get Mikey over a small ditch at home. It was an anxiety-inducing experience for all, and I genuinely hated every minute of it. When we were done, Mikey was sweaty and amped up, I was in tears, and my instructors looked exhausted. Knowing what I know now, I would have handled teaching him about the ditch very differently—starting from the ground, taking my time, breaking it down into much smaller steps, and working under the philosophy that "we don't have to get over it today." I am certain a different approach would have left us both feeling much better about the ditch and about each other.

Despite the challenges, however, Mikey and I had quite a bit of success at the regional show jumping and eventing rallies that summer. Then it was time for my A-level test. I honestly felt incredibly well-prepared, having done several prep clinics with the toughest Pony Club examiner in the region and leaving those sessions with confidence. So Mikey and I joined five other A-level hopefuls at a farm in upstate New York in the late summer.

One of the main purposes of the A-level test is to show that a candidate is ready to be a horse trainer, not just a rider. To that end, part of my test included "catch rides" on unknown horses, and we were to discuss what we were feeling and working on in the saddle with the examiner. The farm where the five other candidates and I were taking our test had horses on site for us to use for the catch-ride portion of the exam. We rode in whatever tack the horses were brought to us in, which added a layer of complexity—say, if the saddle didn't fit us, or the bit choice wasn't one we were comfortable with.

The first catch-ride horse I sat on was simple enough, and I must have explained what I was doing in a satisfactory way, because the examiner seemed pleased and suggested a horse swap between me and another candidate. While riding that first horse, I had, of course, eyeballed the other horses and riders in the arena. My second mount had looked pretty well-schooled when I'd watched him go, but when I got on, I could feel immediately how behind the leg the horse was and realized that his first rider had been doing *a lot* of work. So I put on my "trainer hat" and thought about how I would handle the horse's issues for his long-term success, not just how I would make him "look pretty" for the next fifteen minutes. After all, I was meant to be a trainer now, not just a rider. I went about the process of "legging him up" in the way that Steve and I had worked on countless times: *light aid, no response, light correction with the stick, leg off, start again.* I repeated this process methodically until I started to feel the horse respond to my light leg aid. I was not concerned with his shape in the bridle nor his acceptance of the bit, because I did not want to muddy the horse's understanding of going *forward* with any pressure from my reins. I didn't want to end up in a contradictory "kicking and pulling" situation, and I didn't want to have to work so hard with my legs to put him in a round package to my hands. I simply wanted to check the box of "response to my leg" before I moved on to "finding a connection to the bridle."

Forward first. Leg before hand. Dressage Training 101.

I hadn't worked on this process for long when the examiner asked me to give an explanation of what I was doing. I did, similarly to the way in which I just explained it here, and she asked a few questions, which I answered with my same training philosophy in mind. I felt confident it was the right process for the horse in that moment, from a training perspective. And I would stand by that today.

After the catch-ride phase of the exam was over, the examiner took each test participant aside to discuss their performance and indicate whether they had passed or failed. The first two riders looked relieved after their brief conversations with the examiner. They had clearly passed. I was full of confidence in my process and explanation of it as I joined the examiner for my results. I was *totally and completely* unprepared for her to tell me that I had failed the catch-ride section of the A-level test.

The examiner told me I had not shown the full capability of the second horse well enough during my time riding him. I knew this assessment was made in comparison to how the other candidate had ridden the horse. Without negating the work of the other candidate, I wanted to explain again that I had been filling a training gap in the horse's understanding of basic flatwork. But I couldn't find the right words, and I knew there was no point in arguing anyway. The other rider had made the horse look better than I had, and it seemed that was all that mattered to the examiner. She had already made her call, and there was no going back. I was also on the verge of tears, so I could not have spoken clearly if I had tried. I felt like I had been punched in the gut.

The examiner told me I could continue with the rest of the test if I wanted to, but I was devastated, and knew I was in no shape to ride a horse. I also knew that because of my age and the relative infrequency of when A-level tests are offered, there would be no opportunity for me to retake the catch-ride portion of the test, even if I passed every other section.

So that was that. I never even rode Mikey in New York. My mom and boyfriend, who had accompanied me, helped me pack up all the things we had so recently unpacked, and we drove home.

I was so ashamed. I was also angry. Maybe I just wasn't good enough. But I knew I had a better understanding of training theory and process than some of the other riders I had tested with. I also knew there was nothing I could do about the results. I felt powerless, livid, and embarrassed. I cried when I explained what had happened to Steve, and he agreed that I had demonstrated and explained how to train that particular horse correctly. After talking it over with him, I knew that I would handle the ride the same way if I was back there again, even knowing how it would turn out (with me failing), because that was the right step for that particular horse's understanding. But that didn't make me feel any better when I had to tell person after person what had happened.

A few weeks after the test, a local vet who rode with Virginia came to try Mikey. She loved him and bought him (and kept him until he died, many happy years later). I fulfilled my promise to his owner and her parents, sending them the profits from his sale before I headed back to school.

For years after the rating fiasco, even after I'd left Connecticut behind, I told people who asked that I never got to take my A-level test because I never had the horse for it. I did this mostly because I was too embarrassed to simply tell people I had failed. I also didn't want to go through the process of explaining what had happened, as I didn't want to come across like a know-it-all. I always knew, though, that Mikey *was* the horse for it. I just never got the chance to prove it.

The endeavor of trying to earn my A rating held several life lessons for me. The biggest was acknowledging that sometimes you have to choose a process over "looking pretty" in the moment, because it's the right thing to do in the long term. I would learn time and again this could be very hard to stick to in high-pressure situations, such as those in front of other people or in competitive spaces. But horse shows and clinics are isolated moments in the course of a horse's career. The bulk of training happens in between those events and is an accumulation of all the little moments you are in contact with a horse. *It's not all going to look pretty.* Every one of us has had to fumble our way, ungracefully, through learning new things in our lives—horses too. Sometimes growth is messy, and when you try to gloss over the mess to make sure it looks a certain way from the outside, you will inevitably be leaving some ugly stuff bubbling underneath that will eventually come to the surface.

For that catch-ride horse, and horses like him, he might have never advanced to real collection on the flat because he never truly worked from his own engine or carried his own balance. Or he might have lost confidence and stopped at fences because he didn't believe his rider when asked to move forward to a better distance. These are both typical issues that tend to surface with horses that are chronically behind the leg. They have a way of manifesting at some point in time, just like our own personal issues that we bury rather than work on. They rear their ugly heads at inopportune moments because we don't address them when they first appear, because we want to look like we "have it all together." But if we are striving for successful long-term outcomes, we are better off taking the time to work on things more slowly and methodically, checking for true understanding in ourselves and our equine partners—onlookers and examiners be damned.

Failing my catch-ride test was also one of my first encounters with the effects of shame. Shame is the feeling that you, as a person, are deeply flawed when something goes wrong in your life, rather than being able to separate your identity from that situation. I had a hard time telling people the truth about failing my rating because I thought it reflected on me as a person. *Who would still like me if they knew? Who would want to hire me to help with their horses? Who would think I'm worthy of their time and attention? Maybe I really am not good enough.*

This has been a recurring theme in my life with horses. I couldn't see it then, but I do in hindsight, even as I still work with the pieces of me that struggle with shame. It's a tough one to eradicate.

8
FINDING OPPORTUNITY

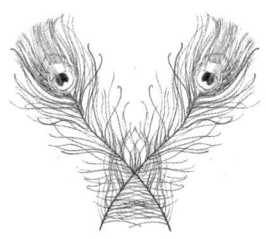

AFTER A YEAR AND A HALF at the University of Connecticut, I decided to study abroad for a semester with a friend and boyfriend through a program based in Maynooth, Ireland. I had amazing experiences that semester, exploring the many coastal towns and natural phenomena of Ireland and Northern Ireland as well as traveling to the Netherlands, Italy, and Greece during the long spring break. Through my participation in the intercollegiate riding team at Maynooth, I made friends to whom I am still connected, to this day. I *will* say that I have never seen so much alcohol consumption paired with riding as I did during those months, and I was even more surprised that it wasn't something students hid from the adults. Everyone partook, and some hilarious, though admittedly risky, memories were made.

The biggest thing my semester in Ireland did for me was spark a sense of adventure. As our time in Maynooth drew to an end, I had no desire to go back to Connecticut, having finally left it. I made up my mind to look at schools in different states and to transfer after the summer break. My mom worried about this decision but didn't protest, so I started my search.

My new college search criteria included an institution in a state I had never been to, preferably near an ocean, and that would offer me scholarships. I applied to three different schools in Florida, and the University of West Florida in Pensacola gave me the best financial package. With my mom's reluctant approval, and a friend of a friend willing to help drive a moving truck with my car in tow, I made my way south to finish my Bachelor of Fine Art degree. My mom helped me rent my very first apartment, which I furnished with hand-me-downs, Goodwill finds, and Dollar Store purchases. It was strange and exciting to be on my own, and also a bit lonely, so it wasn't long before I adopted my first dog to keep me company. I called her Angel and told people she was a French Beagle, a breed I totally made up but sounded rare and fancy. She was my constant companion and helped me connect with new people, as friendly dogs often do.

Knowing how important having horses in my life was to my mental health, my mom also helped me find a local barn where I could ride in exchange for barn work. As had been the case at the UConn Morgan facility, the farm owner was pleasantly surprised to find that I actually seemed to know how to ride a horse, and he gave me the opportunity to work with several he didn't have time for. I was promised instruction, though I received very little, but I was nonetheless happy to have specific horses to play with on a regular basis in a way that let me see progress with them.

My favorite was Bunny, a sensitive mare that no one else seemed to much enjoy being around. I got on well with the sensitive animals, and I began to find I could settle their worries in ways that seemed to surprise other people. Now I recognize that having clarity and consistency in my aids was a tenet I lived by, and horses took comfort in working with me because they knew what to expect and when they had answered my questions correctly. This is a skill I try to help everyone I teach develop, as it is so paramount to a clear conversation between horse and rider, and it can be absolutely pivotal in improving their relationship. Thankfully it's also a skill that can be learned with diligent and focused practice. *Feel* and *timing* can be taught, despite what many people say about them being innate skills that you either have or you don't. Sure, there are people with a more natural ability to feel what a horse needs, moment to moment, and to respond to the horse without having to think their way through the process. But anyone who is willing to put in the effort to better these skills can do it. It just takes time and commitment to the process.

Horse farm owners are *always* looking for help; therefore, if you're a horse person who is willing to work hard, you will always find a place to land. But no matter how much you think you know, you can't go into farmwork scenarios expecting owners and trainers to just give you lessons and nice horses to ride. You have to earn it. You have to be willing to get your hands dirty and shovel shit. You have to be willing to show up early and stay late. You have to work with whatever horses you're handed (with your own safety in mind, of course) and not be bitter when somebody else gets an opportunity with a horse you think is a nicer ride. You have to work your way up. You have to be willing to learn and take advice from other trainers, owners, and farm workers. Respect and privileges are earned; proving you are trustworthy and responsible through your actions over time is how you earn them. It's not always going to be fun. You're not always going to enjoy the horses that you are working with. But every ride on every horse is an opportunity to learn something—about what you like or don't like, about a new technique or tool for your toolbox, about a philosophy or process that works well for a certain type of horse or rider. It all goes into making you a more well-rounded horse person, and human, in the long run.

There weren't any peers at the farm that I felt particularly drawn to, and the established riders and staff seemed cold toward me, which I thought was maybe because the farm owner, who was also the head trainer, gave me a lot of freedom and opportunity. I wanted to avoid the drama and conflict that I could feel brewing, so I kept my head down, did my work, and rode the horses I was allowed to ride, relying on the horses at the farm for companionship rather than the people. Thankfully, I made a group of friends in the art department at the University of West Florida, and my social life quickly improved. I also played my "Pony Club card" and found a local club that was happy to have my help with lessons, ratings, and camps. This brought me a bit of income and provided additional opportunities, including the chance to teach at a summer camp in Saint Croix, one of the US Virgin Islands in the Caribbean.

Teaching camp in Saint Croix, where there is still a well-established, long-standing Pony Club, was one of the most amazing experiences of my life with horses. The amount of responsibility that was put in my hands, not only with the vehicle and house rentals they arranged, but also with the instruction I was asked to give the students, was daunting to live up to and affirming at the same time. The farm owners in Saint Croix did the best with what they had, and I was impressed with how well-cared-for the horses seemed to be. They were all appropriate mounts for their riders, and were all relaxed enough with their island life to take us on beach rides and swims in the ocean. I developed a deep desire to leave a lasting impact on the horses and kids there, knowing how limited their access to regular instruction was. I wanted them to leave camp with skills they didn't know they needed, but once they'd learned them, couldn't imagine riding without. I hoped I could leave them with new understandings and critical thinking skills that would allow them to help themselves and their horses in the absence of other sources of guidance.

My time on the island really opened my eyes to the fact that not everyone in the horse world has access to horsemanship education, in any form. It made me realize I should never underestimate the impact I might have on another aspiring rider. My ideas and suggestions could be the tiny pebbles that get dropped into the pond and cause a lifetime of ripples. I knew there were people who'd had this effect on my life, and even still, it was hard to imagine doing it for someone else. Throughout my past, I have suffered from self-doubt and feelings of impostor syndrome. I've had to remind myself that the people who helped me over the years at one point probably had *their own* self-doubts.

It's also okay to know that you don't know everything, and to offer what you *do* know with that caveat. The minute you think you know everything you are no longer a good teacher, anyway—you are just a mouthpiece for your own agenda. You will miss the lessons that you could learn while trying to impart your own ideas, and you will cease to grow. Any trainer I have ever had who was worth their salt was also a perpetual student. Staying open to learning while teaching others is the only way to be valuable in that role.

Back in Pensacola, I picked up a couple of adult amateur clients through the Pony Club connection I made there. One of them had a nice Thoroughbred who I worked with regularly, and she offered to sign me up to ride her horse in a clinic with international eventer Darren Chiacchia. I had no idea who Darren was at the time, but I soon learned he was on the fast track to the US Olympic Eventing Team headed to Athens with the Trakehner stallion Windfall.

Darren was very kind and complimentary during my clinic lesson with him. At that time, he had a farm in Ocala and offered that if I was ever in the area, I could come for a lesson on one of the horses he kept there. As it happened, my boyfriend Patrick's family was from Ocala, and so when Patrick and I went to see his family over the holidays, I took Darren up on his offer. After my lesson, Darren suggested that if I was ever looking for a "working student" gig, he might be able to bring me on.

At the time I didn't have a horse of my own and was a semester away from finishing my degree, so I tucked his proposal away as a possibility for the future. I was incredibly flattered, though, and knew I *wanted* to take him up on the offer—when I could.

Being singled out and appreciated for your skills feels amazing, and I believe in being open to opportunities, as this openness has led to many unexpected turns of good fortune in my own life. It's also easy to imagine what these opportunities will be like, and then to be sorely disappointed when they are not what you expected. *Embracing opportunity without expectation of a particular outcome* is one of the hardest things to do. We all love to fantasize about what *could* happen and where things *might* lead, but I have found that one of the largest sources of disappointment in my life is being attached to how I think something will turn out, and having it turn out differently.

In this way, "hope" can also be a dangerous temptation. This is a controversial idea, as hope is so often seen as a positive quality. But when we hope, we can easily become attached to a desired outcome, and if that outcome doesn't come to fruition, we will feel more disappointed than if we had left hope out of the equation. It then becomes a process of letting go of the thing we thought we wanted and learning the lessons that have been presented to us instead.

I wonder, if we let go of hope, and instead embrace openness to *all* possibilities, if we would feel less disappointment and more joy and gratitude for what we do have in our lives.

9
FINDING OPENNESS

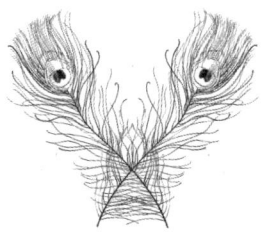

BY THE TIME I graduated college in 2002, I was engaged to Patrick and had a plan to lease a small horse farm in the northeast corner of Tennessee, where I hoped to start a boarding and training business. Patrick had applied to several Master of Fine Art graduate programs, all over the United States, and had not been accepted into any. I would have been willing to follow him wherever he got in, continuing my piecemeal equine journey wherever we landed, but when it became clear that his plan was not going to come to fruition, I put my own in place.

The farm I found had ten stalls, ample turnout, an outdoor riding arena, and an apartment on site. It was located in the tiny town of Laurel Bloomery, Tennessee, right on the Virginia line in the beautiful Blue Ridge mountains. It was owned by a woman named Marilyn Mitchell. The arrangement I made with Marilyn was ideal: She needed help with the horses already at her farm, and there was room for me to bring some in, as well. She had a great eye for quality low-level horses and had a couple of sources for inexpensive ones that she would pick up, put a few months of training into, and then sell. She'd run this system with the help one of her daughters, Amy, but since Amy was off having her own life adventures at the time, Marilyn was happy to have my help while I was building my own business. Her resale projects were an opportunity for me to earn a living, as well as gain a lot of experience. And as was becoming a useful pattern, I also connected with a local Pony Club, and started picking up some lesson clients and horses in training through that association.

My time at Marilyn's was my first real foray into the traditional practices of what most think of as "natural horsemanship." Marilyn gave me my first rope halter, made by a cowboy friend of hers. She showed me the basics of moving a horse's feet around me in a circle and having control over his hind end by disengaging it. She introduced me to a round pen and the idea of a horse "joining up" with me (a term coined by legendary horseman Monty Roberts). I was both fascinated and intrigued. The basics of respectful handling that Steve had given me had their roots in what Marilyn was now expanding on, and I wanted to understand how the work could be applicable to my competitive goals. With the few things that Marilyn showed me, I knew "just enough to be dangerous," but I earnestly wanted to learn what this new world could offer my overall journey with horses.

As I was learning about this new-to-me training methodology, I was connecting with the eventing community of the area. We weren't far from the meccas of the Virginia and Kentucky Horse Parks, as well as smaller USEA-rated events. The Pony Club kids I was teaching all wanted to event, and through one of them, I was literally given a horse to play along with. Her name was Starlet, and she was a ten-year-old chestnut Thoroughbred mare. At the time, I was unaware of the colorful stereotype attached to this description, but boy did Starlet live up to it.

The only thing I was told about this mare was that she had evented through the Preliminary level and her owner needed to "move on" from her. I quickly figured out a few of the probable reasons *why* this might be the case: Starlet didn't know how to stand at a mounting block, preferring to be a quickly moving target for her rider to leap onto, and she had a propensity for rearing during dressage tests. But she would also jump anything I put in front of her, and despite her quirks, most days I felt like I had won the lottery. I had never had a horse that had such an easy time on cross-country. Starlet allowed me to get some real-world eventing experience under my belt.

During my time at Marilyn's, Patrick and I were to be married. The wedding was set for the fall of 2003 at a beautiful resort in North Carolina, where my family from both New England and the West Coast and Patrick's family from the South would all converge. My best friend from my childhood, Alyssa, flew in to help me with last-minute preparations in Tennessee before we would drive to the wedding site together.

I was excited about my newly acquired natural horsemanship skills, and I wanted to show them off to Alyssa when she arrived. I brought her and a sweet older horse named Teddy out to the round pen so that I could impress her with the "joining up" process. I intended to show her the way Teddy would seem to ignore me at first and then magically end up following me around like a dog.

But things didn't go as easily as I had hoped. Teddy did not join up quickly. Instead, he spent a fair bit of time distractedly running around the perimeter of the round pen at my urging. My very limited knowledge told me to keep him moving and turning until he looked at me. I know now that I wasn't really watching his body language, and that even if I *had* been totally focused on him, I would not have known what I was looking for. Instead, I felt a perceived pressure with my friend watching, and I was embarrassed at how long things were taking. I tried to cover up my lack of understanding by applying more pressure, having Teddy move faster and change directions more often. Eventually, Teddy did stop running and came a bit closer to me. He was sweaty and puffing, so I called it a day.

The silly thing was, my friend was *not* a horse person and had *no idea* what was supposed to happen. Nor can I imagine that she cared, other than to humor her "horse girl" friend. Nonetheless, I was exceedingly embarrassed by my and Teddy's performance, and tried to distract myself by moving on to happier things, like arranging centerpieces for the wedding.

Later that evening, Marilyn knocked on the door to our apartment, which was a very rare event. I had never seen her mad before, and I was shocked to find that when I opened the door, her *very real* anger was directed at me. She informed me that as a result of our round pen session earlier that day, Teddy had scraped up his legs and was swollen everywhere and extremely uncomfortable. Marilyn was furious on Teddy's behalf, and rightly so. I hadn't cared for Teddy properly. I had been so busy trying to show off for my friend that I had forgotten about the horse's welfare.

I was ashamed and apologetic, but Marilyn was not in a place to accept my apology, and she left the apartment in a huff. It was a very depressing and uncomfortable way to finish preparations for what was supposed to be one of the happiest days of my life. Alyssa tried to cheer me up, pointing out that everyone makes mistakes, but my guilt and shame were overwhelming. How could I claim to love horses the way I did and have put Teddy in that position? It was something I couldn't let go of easily—I assumed it reflected on me as both a trainer *and* a person. I was very worried about how it would affect my working relationship with Marilyn, as well.

Anything you do with a horse can be done poorly. I don't care if it's natural horsemanship, traditional training, positive reinforcement, or the latest in healing bodywork—we humans can mess it up. We miss signals. We are distracted, spinning our wheels in our own minds when we should be watching our horses. We communicate our desires poorly.

That's on us.

Horses never asked to be part of the human world, and they give us so much that we take for granted in the day-to-day hustle and bustle of our lives. If you stop to think about the extraordinary nature of our relationships with horses, it's completely mind-blowing. These graceful, empathic creatures allow us to ask more of them than most prey animals on the planet would ever be able to handle, and even when we make mistakes that make their lives harder, they let us try again. They allow us to dress them up in ridiculous outfits and parade them around sandboxes and jump them over things they could much more easily go around, all for our pleasure and entertainment. They ignore their instincts at our request. They give us the opportunity to reflect on our own habits and behaviors and to become better versions of ourselves, simply by the nature of their being in this world.

Horses have no desire to work in the ways *we* think are fun or beautiful. If left to their own devices, they would be happy to graze all day and relate to their own species over ours. But they are creatures of least resistance. They seek to conserve energy and exist in as peaceful a way as possible in order to survive. Most of what we do with them is about *meeting our own needs*. I'm not saying this is wrong—I can't imagine my life without training horses. But anything a horse does that a human might deem as *in*correct, I have to assume is *on me* in some way. *I need* to do a better job of breaking down information and understanding my end goal for the horse. *I need* to clarify and be consistent enough in my processes that my horse understands me, despite the language barrier between us. I can't come to a horse with my own ego and needs at the forefront and expect a positive result, even if I think I'm applying "gentle" techniques. This will *always* end with the horse on the losing side.

Understanding this in a deep way has made it easier for me to be patient with both the horses and people I work with, and to forgive myself when I make inevitable human mistakes.

The wedding a few days later was beautiful, and everyone seemed to have a wonderful time, including Marilyn (thankfully). But in my heart, leading up to and even during the ceremony, I knew that something was not right.

I was aware that I was doing the "next thing" that most people do when in a relationship for a long time, but I had a sinking feeling that things would end badly for me with Patrick. As it was, I was on a moving train that I couldn't stop, so the ceremony and reception happened, and I came away from the weekend a married woman and went off on a honeymoon cruise with my new husband.

We returned five days later to the devastating news that my grandfather, a man I was very close to and who I had just danced with at my wedding, had died of cardiac arrest a few hours after returning home after the reception. It was a time before extended cell phone range, and there had been no way for my family to reach us on the ship. The funeral had been held the day before we got back. To say I was shocked was an understatement.

Once home, I was overcome by a sense of numbness and guilt like I had never felt before. I had married Patrick, even though I felt doubt about going through with it. And then my grandfather, who had traveled by car to celebrate with us, had died, exhausted from the journey. Deep down I knew that it wasn't actually my fault that he had passed, but I couldn't help but wonder, if he hadn't made that trip, would he still be alive?

My heart was heavy as I began work again at the farm in Tennessee. Marilyn had taken in a couple of rescue horses, one of which was an older mare whose life story was written in the scars on her body. She was sweet as the tea that everyone drank in Tennessee, and I couldn't imagine how someone could have treated her so poorly. I also couldn't believe how willing she was to be around people, considering what it was clear she had been through.

Around this time, I was also introduced to one of Marilyn's neighbors who was a reiki practitioner. I had watched him work on the horses at the farm, and I was curious about the process. Given my experience at Lost Run Farm after the sage-burning, I wondered if I might be sensitive enough to learn things about the mare if I mimicked what I had seen the neighbor doing with other horses.

I brought the sweet horse onto the cross-ties one afternoon when we were alone in the barn. I took a deep breath, closed my eyes, and raised my hands to the scars along her neck, hovering a few inches above her coat and breathing slow, deep breaths. About ten seconds into the experiment, I felt a rush of fear, pain, and sadness flood my body through my hands. I gasped out loud and stepped back quickly from the mare, who hadn't moved a muscle, shaking my hands as I pulled them away from her. In an instant, I had tears streaming uncontrollably down my cheeks, and no explanation for any of what had just transpired. I immediately called Marilyn and relayed the story. She, in turn, reached out to her neighbor, who came over right away to "finish" what I had started, both for me and for the horse.

Thankfully, no one was upset with my dalliance with reiki—they were more surprised by my sensitivity than anything. For me, the experience was another step toward becoming aware of things unseen but felt deeply. It conveyed clearly to me that horses have messages to tell us that they have no means of communicating. It made me both anxious and excited to have what I considered proof of this, and I felt determined to be the voice for every horse I came into contact with from then on.

My experience with the rescue mare and the conversations I had with Marilyn and her neighbor afterward led me to truly believe that even when horses are "quiet" and outwardly seem relaxed, there may be things under the surface they have to say. It's up to us, as individuals, to find out the best ways to uncover and understand that information. There are a million "healing" modalities in the equine world, and I don't believe that there is one that fits every scenario—people are different, horses are different, situations are different. Who am I to say that an animal communicator can't help you have a better relationship with your horse, or that Magnawave or massage can't improve your horse's performance? If it helps you, and you feel a palpable difference in your time with your horse as a result, use whatever modality available to you with your horse. I've had too many experiences in my life that I cannot explain to judge another's beliefs about the unseen world. There will always be treatment options that demonstrate results with scientific evidence. I have also seen studies used to shore up claims that could be proven false if different evidence was taken into consideration. And I know there are avenues of treatment that create results that can't be quantified as clearly, but that people swear by.

To each their own. Who am I to judge?

10
FINDING TOUGHNESS

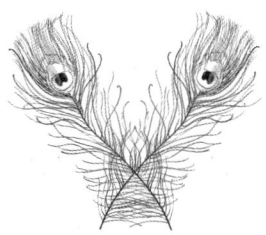

THE INTANGIBLE was very much in play in my work with Starlet, although in an entirely different context. As I mentioned before, I hadn't known there were jokes about her "type" when Starlet was given to me, but soon after, somebody gifted me a bumper sticker that read, *Hell hath no fury like a chestnut Thoroughbred mare.*

Starlet proved that sticker right.

This mare was quiet and sweet as honey one moment, and then all fire and unpredictability the next. She could go around like a Warmblood, swinging her back and carrying herself beautifully, or she could drop her back, hollow her neck, and stand on two legs at the drop of a hat. She could lope around a course like a children's hunter, or she could bolt around a course like an unbroke youngster, tossing rails aside like pick-up sticks.

She was clearly a castoff. She couldn't move up the levels in the eventing world because of her unpredictable emotional outbursts, and probably also because of her physical stature. She was only about 15.1 hands tall and very finely built, and could lean toward tension in her work, occasionally exhibiting dangerous behavior. But she was also a horse who was talented enough for me to take Darren Chiacchia up on his working student offer without being laughed off the farm.

I arranged to go to Darren's place for three months. My new in-laws still lived in Ocala, and I could stay with them while I worked at Darren's farm. So I loaded Starlet into a little old bumper-pull trailer, and we made our way south from Tennessee.

We arrived without ceremony or fanfare, and I started regular shifts the next morning with no real formal arrangement about hours, other than I would be working every day and I would get lessons as often as possible. After watching me school Starlet on the flat, Darren commented in a very surprised tone that Starlet and I could actually do pretty nice flatwork. I don't think he'd expected much from us when I'd unloaded her from our meager rig! But when Starlet was "on," her gaits were lovely and we made a pretty pair. And she definitely had some springs, so jumping was a no-brainer for her. After discussing a three-month plan with Darren, I set my sights on moving up to Training level by the end of our time in Florida.

My stint at Darren's was pretty typical of a working student gig, with long hours, some riding instruction, some opportunity to ride other horses, and a chance to rub elbows with the movers and shakers of the eventing world. I made friends with my fellow working students and Darren's head groom, Kristin. She introduced me to other grooms, including Max Corcoran, who was the head groom for Olympic eventing couple David and Karen O'Connor at the time. Kristen taught me how to ride a motorbike to get around at horse shows, and played mediator between Darren, his clients, and his working students. She was the organizer of all things and had a calm demeanor that balanced Darren's high energy. She was a friend to everyone, and didn't spend time on gossip. Kristin clearly loved the horses she cared for, especially Windfall, and took tending to their needs very seriously. Darren clearly trusted her implicitly, and she set a wonderful example of what a head groom and farm manager should be. I was very grateful for her presence and guidance.

It's fair to say that the concepts and practices of natural horsemanship I had started to learn from Marilyn did not play a real role at an upper-level eventing facility in those days, and it felt a bit more like the farms where I'd grown up riding. There was a certain comfort for me in that. But I also couldn't shake the feeling that certain decisions were made that didn't sit right with me—for example, a horse being asked to continue working and competing at a very high level, despite a clear degenerative condition. The horse was being treated and was well cared for, but he also remained on the competitive circuit because he was talented and still "trying" for his rider. For me, the willingness to try didn't necessarily mean the horse was still comfortable in the work.

And there was a night Darren had some friends over for a dinner party, and he introduced me as "the one with the gorgeous husband." It seemed to me he had clearly forgotten my name in the moment, and I was terribly uncomfortable with being more memorable for the outward appearance of my spouse than I was for any other quality that he could think of. I laughed awkwardly at the introduction, shrinking into myself for the rest of the dinner. I was beginning to feel like just another cog in a machine that the horses were also part of—small and replaceable. A piece of me desperately wanted to be a more important part of that machine, and another piece of me wanted *out*, immediately.

When it came time for our move up to Training level at Rocking Horse Farm, near the end of our scheduled stay at Darren's, I felt that Starlet and I were ready, and from what I could tell, Darren seemed to think so too. We put in a pretty darn good dressage test (with zero rearing!), and despite a rail in show jumping, had a double clean cross-country run, landing us just inside the ribbons in eighth place. I was thrilled with our results, riding against a large field of "real" competitors at my first big event, but when I told Darren the news, he told me that if it wasn't blue, it didn't mean anything.

I was devastated, having been expecting at least some words of advice about how to improve our next time out. I tried not to let anyone see me crying, but a kind and clearly talented young man who had been with Darren for many months more than I had comforted me, and we commiserated about how harsh it was for working students. I felt absolutely awful, but I didn't think I had another choice if I wanted to be part of the upper-level eventing world. I assumed I would have to toughen up to make it.

My time in Ocala ended a little sooner than expected after a young horse stepped on my foot while I was blanketing him, twisted his hoof on top of my paddock boot, and almost fully removed my left big toenail—not a pleasant experience! I was unable to do the kind of work that was necessary to remain a working student, so Starlet and I headed back to Tennessee a couple of weeks early. Darren made no effort to wish me well or say goodbye; it was another moment in which I remember feeling easily disposed of and replaced, as I knew another working student would be there soon to take over the role I was vacating. Part of me was disappointed for my time in a barn of that caliber to be ending, and another part was ready to leave being a working student far behind.

The working student "factory" can be demoralizing and disheartening for so many, in the same way it was for me. I gave up on the system after my time at Darren's, but I have since seen that if a person finds the right place, such an apprenticeship can be worth every moment and every bit of effort that you put into it. I can also say now, having learned from my own mistakes, that if the position you find yourself in doesn't feel right, it probably *isn't*. If you're losing confidence instead of gaining it, then you're probably in the wrong place with the wrong people. If you feel more anxious at the end of most days than you do at the beginning, that's a sign that something's not right. We want our horses to become more relaxed and gain confidence and understanding in our sessions with them; a student should do the same under the tutelage of the right teacher. Sure, there will be tough moments of growth and discomfort when stretching to learn new things, but the overall arc should be one of positive experiences tending toward *lowered* stress levels and higher confidence.

This doesn't mean you won't work your ass off as a working student! That's part of the deal. But declining emotional health should not be. Some people out there will say I just wasn't tough enough to be a working student at a farm with that caliber of high-level work. But I am still deeply embedded in the horse world, *not* because of my working student experience, but *despite it*. Many people who I know were considered "tougher" than me at the time I rode at Darren's are no longer involved with horses professionally or personally. To me, true toughness doesn't mean being a doormat. It doesn't mean shutting up and taking it because "that's the price of learning under the best." It means knowing and valuing yourself enough to get out of a situation that has the potential to dissuade you from your larger goals and seeking a place that encourages you to reach them.

I try to be a launch point for any working student I take into my program. I try to see them as individuals with their own personal goals, not just laborers to help me reach mine. I try to stay open enough to consider what I might learn from *them*, even as I try to impart my own knowledge of horses and training during our time together. When I can do this well, I have been pleasantly surprised by the lively discussion and self-reflection their questions and input have provoked in me.

My first attempt to be a working student was so detrimental to my confidence, I didn't think my psyche or my self-esteem could take any more "tough love." I knew I wanted to work with horses for the rest of my life, and at that time, I thought I wanted to do this as an upper-level event rider. So Starlet and I made our own way on the eventing circuit of the southeastern United States with very little instruction or help along the way. We did quite well when she could keep it together during the dressage phase, and we were out of the ribbons when she couldn't.

Our second season together, Starlet and I qualified for the American Eventing Championships at Training level. The event was held at the Carolina Horse Park, and on day one, we were putting in a lovely dressage test when a group of Comanche helicopters from the nearby Air Force base flew low over the dressage arena, right in the middle of our free walk. Starlet's understandable response to stand on her hind legs, then spin and try to flee the scene, took us well out of the running for a top placing there, even with clean show jumping and cross-country runs. It was very frustrating that we were so unlucky as to have the helicopters fly over during our test, and that there was no "do-over" allowed for such an unusual occurrence. But I was proud of our efforts together nonetheless.

Starlet and I competed together for another year or so, moving up to the preliminary level and having moderate success, but mostly putting competition miles under my belt. At some point during our third season together, I started to sense that Starlet was truly unhappy doing the job I was asking her to do. Her erratic behavior in dressage tests bled over into our warm-ups and became more regular. It seemed that the pressure of the competitive space was overwhelming her ability to hear my attempts at quiet communication.

I used every resource I had in my toolbox at that time, but things didn't get better. So I made the decision to stop competing Starlet. She transitioned into the role of "lesson horse," and I was able to teach some advanced-beginner students on her. She proved herself to be quite a responsible babysitter for the right riders in my program. I knew that because of her history and volatility I couldn't in good conscience put Starlet back into a situation where another rider might compete with her, so to me, selling her was out of the question.

Starlet seemed to most enjoy long hacks out in the Tennessee mountain woods. I got myself a lightweight synthetic Western saddle that Starlet's delicate frame could carry easily. I would throw a rope halter on her, and off we would go onto the trails behind the farm, up and down the steep inclines and over the many streams—for hours, just the two of us. It was quiet, save the sounds of the natural world around us: chirping birds and wind in the trees as Starlet's sure-footed steps guided us over the rocky terrain. I have never been one who loves trail riding, but the way Starlet would march out onto those trails with a relaxed purpose in her step, stress-free and ready to take on the world in front of her, brought me a joy that made what she loved to do fun for both of us.

Sometimes, with a horse or in life, you just have to start over the best way you know how. The more I learned about Starlet's history, the more it made sense that she had been given to me. Clearly, her former owner had been unable to continue competing her because she was sometimes impossible to even get in the ring. Despite my limited toolbox, I must have done something right with the mare, because she and I did have a good bit of success. I used the tools I *did* have to help rewrite her understanding of the horse-human relationship. I applied less pressure than I am sure she had been used to, and I made my appreciation of her "try" clear in the timing and degree of my releases. I varied her routine to include things like trail rides. I didn't show her more than once per month, about six or seven times a year. And most importantly, I didn't go into every interaction with Starlet assuming she was going to be a naughty horse. I simply rode what she was each day.

There were a couple of times that I remember when Starlet and I really butted heads, and in those moments, I dipped deep into our "relationship bank," removing most of the accumulated funds to get my message across the best way I knew how. I would then work hard to replenish those funds in the following days and weeks, and to listen to her when she told me she needed a break.

Unless what you are doing with a horse is abusive, causing harm to his body or mind, please rest assured that *your best* is enough for now. At the same time, make it your mission in life to add new tools to your toolbox every single day. Figure out if you need to work on yourself and your emotional regulation or ability to be present with your horse, or if you need help with training techniques and theories. If you think you may have damaged your horse's physical or emotional well-being, be even more adamant in your search for new understanding. Don't be afraid to start over. Go back to absolute scratch and get help rebuilding from the foundation up. Believe me, it will be worth the time it takes. Starlet's former owner didn't or couldn't take the time the mare required to rebuild, so she sent her along to me. That was probably the best outcome, because what Starlet needed at that time in her life didn't align with her former owner's goals. It was not a right or wrong situation, a good or bad situation—it was just a personal choice.

I have found it is sometimes kinder to let a relationship go than it is to keep trying to fit a square peg into a round hole. And if you *aren't* ready to move on from a tumultuous relationship with a horse, you have to be willing to slow down and start over with him, and stop wishing your horse or the situation were different than it is. You have to prioritize "putting funds in your relationship bank," and if you're not sure how to do that, you need to learn how to from someone who does.

It is a Buddhist belief that one root of suffering is the unwillingness to accept *what is*, along with the constant wish that things be other than they are. I am not saying that acceptance of *what is* is easy. It may be accompanied by disappointment, feelings of deep loss, and the process of grieving *what might have been*. I think, though, that it is less difficult and painful in the long run than beating your head against the same wall for years.

A couple of years after retiring Starlet from competition, my mom and I went on a trip for her fiftieth birthday to Sedona, Arizona, where we went on a multi-night riding trip out into the desert. There I formed a friendship with an older cowboy named Scott, who was our guide through the famous red rocks of the area. I went back to Arizona the following year and had another wonderful adventure with Scott, and it was then I asked him if he thought Starlet would make a useful addition to his string of reliable trail horses. I gave him her whole history—the good, the bad, and the ugly—and told him how much she loved our forays together into the mountains. He took me up on my offer to give Starlet to him, even though he had never had a Thoroughbred in his herd.

So I sent my chestnut mare across the country, and then kept tabs on her through my regular communication with Scott over the next couple of years. Starlet ended up being his personal ride, as she was very sure-footed, energetic, and reliable, but a little too hot for most of the people who he took out into the desert. I gradually lost track of them both, with dwindling contact over time, but I like to think that Starlet lived out her remaining years doing something she enjoyed with a man I knew to be a gentle and understanding soul who admittedly preferred the company of horses to people.

11

FINDING FORGIVENESS

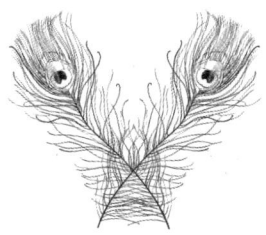

IT WAS DIFFICULT to get clients to come to Marilyn's farm in Tennessee. It was way off the beaten path and tricky in terms of training, especially in the winter, as it had no indoor. Some winters, weather allowed for riding in the outdoor arena the whole season, but sometimes we had snow and ice that didn't melt for weeks, making anything other than walking horses impossible. Since my training business wasn't as lucrative as I'd hoped, I picked up a winter bartending gig in a nearby town, as many young horse people trying to make a name for themselves are known to do in order to make ends meet.

One random weekday evening, a man sat down at the bar during my shift and began to tell me about his most recent financial venture, which was clearly producing a fair bit of stress in his life, prompting him to have a drink before heading home to his wife and kids. He'd just bought a horse farm just across the state border in Virginia, but he had no idea what to do with it. He admitted that he basically bought it for the house on the property, and because his wife and daughter were horse crazy, and he was now trying to figure out how to make it a lucrative business to help pay the substantial mortgage. He and his wife were interested in running it as a boarding barn, but they had no idea where to begin.

I told him I knew just the person for the job.

I sat down formally with John and Andrea, these new husband-and-wife farm owners, and we devised a business plan that involved me moving my training business to their facility and running a boarding barn for them. Patrick and I made the move, and I started running Abingdon Equestrian Center, thankfully with Marilyn's blessing. Her daughter Amy had moved back to the farm, so she had help from family again, and she knew I needed a space with more potential for growth.

The new farm was in a great location, right in the town of Abingdon, which made the pastures small, but the business big. The barn was full before I knew it, and I was working my butt off seven days a week to do the majority of the chores myself, teach as many lessons as I could every day, and ride as many training horses as I could fit in. It was an exhausting schedule, but I was incredibly proud of our flourishing business.

Pretty early on during my time in Abingdon, I met a wonderful woman named Caroline. She had a love for horses that she had put aside for many years to raise her family and start her own business. She was at a point where her children were old enough, and her business was successful enough, that she could put some time and resources into her own passions again. She started taking lessons at my barn and ended up leasing one of my favorite horses of all time, Fizzy. He was an oddly put-together Thoroughbred that I had been privileged to catch-ride some when I was a teenager. After his eventing career had slowed down, his owner, Nancy—my former Pony Club District Commissioner and one of my all-time loudest and most consistent cheerleaders—had asked me if Fizzy would be an asset to my lesson program, knowing that I would give him a wonderful home for the rest of his life, and that we could benefit from each other in his later years. I'd immediately agreed and bought him for a dollar.

A brief aside about Caroline, whose important role in my life cannot be overstated: within a few years of our first meeting, she began the process of designing and building her own private facility a bit farther north in Virginia, in a little town called Wytheville. She was a self-made woman with intelligence and grit that brought her the kind of success that allowed her to follow her dreams in the way so many horse-crazy people can only imagine. I am so lucky that she walked into my barn, and that she remained one of my closest friends and most wonderful clients for my entire time in the South. I eventually ran her private farm, and Fizzy lived out a long life there, being loved and cared for impeccably for more years than any of us ever expected.

Caroline was my student, but also one of my greatest teachers. We had more than a few long, philosophical conversations about life and family and horses, and the sometimes-messy intersection of the three. She was my saving emotional grace on many occasions, and I value every second that I got to spend with her. I have often wondered what my life would have been like if I had stayed at her farm longer than I did, knowing that she provided me with what most young professionals would consider a dream come true...a top-notch facility, lovely horses to ride, and a mentally stable owner who backed the operation. That was not the life I chose, every so often to my regret and dismay, though I am happy to say that Caroline is someone I know I can still call when I need advice about parenting, finances, or family dynamics—or just to reminisce and have a good laugh.

In Abingdon, I had a sense that I knew a good bit more about horses than many of the trainers in the area, but I didn't know how much I still *didn't* know. I was back to being a big fish in a small pond, and I admit I had a chip on my shoulder about it. I had a new plan to "make it" in the eventing world. I got some people to invest in a couple of horses that I planned to move up the levels, and I had deep secret hopes that with these horses, I would get noticed and brought into that inner circle of upper-level event riders I hungered to be part of. I worked constantly and competed at least twice per month all over the Southeast.

Looking back, I know I pushed some of the horses I had in training too hard during that time, because I was convinced that my process was right. I had no room for subtlety or the understanding of horses as individuals with needs that might not fit into the "training box" I was trying to cram them into. As a result, I can see now that I *caused* some problems rather than solving them. When these problems arose, I tried to explain them away as character flaws in the horses, to myself and to their owners, when in reality, it was my own inability to see *my role in the problems* that left them unsolved. I *clearly* did not know what I did not know, and the horses paid the price. I had forgotten the vow I had made to be the voice for the horses I was working with.

My career and my competitive goals were the most important things in my life then. And given my doubts before our wedding, it's not a surprise that my marriage to Patrick fell apart. For sure, he played his own role in our relationship's demise—he wasn't all that motivated to find his own passions in life as I was pursuing my own, and when I wasn't emotionally or physically available, he sought comfort and connection in another person. By the time I realized what was happening and focused my energy on trying to fix things between us, he had already let go of that possibility. He was not interested in trying to make it better, when I finally was, and he asked for a divorce.

I would not wish divorce on my worst enemy. It was the most painful process I have ever been through in my life. The sense of failure I had at the end of our marriage was worse than any I had ever experienced. I had put myself in that position, and I'd known from the start, on some deeper level, that it would be the final outcome of our relationship. And yet I had gone ahead with the marriage, and now all I had to show for it was heartache and failure for the world to see. My clients, friends, and family were kind, though I know many of them had seen it coming too.

Even though Patrick and I had been very distant for quite some time, I had been a serial monogamist since high school, and I was left reeling at the idea of being alone for the first time since I was a teenager. It was one of the darkest times of my life, but the horses still had to be fed and cleaned up after, and I still had to earn a living by training them. I was not the best version of myself during those months. Considering my emotional turmoil, there was no way I could be usefully present and engaged with anyone but myself, especially with creatures as sensitive as horses. I went through the motions as best I could, wallowing through a depression deeper than I had ever known, and relying on the support of reliable clients and forgiving horses for longer than I wanted to.

This was when I really learned that horses are incredibly forgiving beings…until they can no longer be for their sense of safety and comfort to remain intact. For some, the period of forgiveness for the myriad ways humans mistreat them lasts their entire life. For others, that window is much smaller—only a few weeks or months, or maybe even only a few minutes—before they say no to unfair pressure. I have seen trainers who forever make excuses for their own poor work and lack of knowledge by blaming the horse's character. These are the trainers who only find "success" with horses who have a lifetime of forgiveness to offer, because they can't train those who have a smaller window of forgiveness without hitting roadblocks. They are so rigid in their understanding of horses that they have no room for one that doesn't fit neatly inside it. This was me, for a time, in Abingdon, and I am *so glad* that I started to question my own role in the lives of the horses who seemed to "fail out" of my program. It's about as embarrassing to admit to failing those horses as it is having to admit to failing in a marriage, but acknowledging that stage of my development is the only way I have been able to grow and change for the better.

I think that any person who truly loves another person is capable of forgiveness like a horse, but the human window of tolerance for behavior we deem adverse is generally much smaller than a horse's. As humans, we spend much of our time looking outward at how the problems in our lives are caused by the people and circumstances around us. Everything we're unhappy with in our lives can be pinned on someone or something else. It's a universal habit of the human condition, and it takes a lot of practice and choice to turn one's attention inward instead, to see where we might be the creator of our own unhappiness. I don't just mean in obvious ways—as in, we've made a clear mistake that we can own. I mean in subtler ways, like how we create elaborate stories in our own minds about what we think other people have done to us or how they've treated us poorly. These stories are our fabrications, even if to us they seem rooted in truth. They are not anyone else's stories but ours. The person on the other side of those stories likely has a very different version in their own mind, and a bystander probably a completely unique version in theirs.

I have found in my life that when I loosen my grip on my own stories, I have the opportunity to be open to other possibilities, which is far more enjoyable than assuming others are always working against me. This doesn't mean we should turn into self-deprecating messes. It means we get to *change* our stories. It's not about feeling like a terrible person who should "lie in the bed they have made." It's about recognizing the possibility of positive change in oneself. When we choose a self-reflective path, the relationships with the people in our lives and the horses we love improve. We might find that the ease and flow we seek in our daily pursuits is much closer and more accessible than our moving minds would have us believe. We can only enable true and lasting personal growth when we let go of the idea that the problems we face are because of someone or something outside ourselves, be they human or horse, and we interrupt our habitual patterns with an awareness of the present moment—open, clear, and allowing of endless possibility.

12
FINDING HEART AND TRY

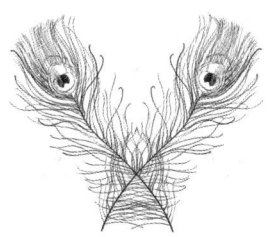

WHILE LIVING IN ABINGDON, I decided to find an inexpensive off-the-track Thoroughbred to bring along the levels of eventing and eventually sell. I was able to gather a group of people to invest up-front capital in such a "project horse" for me, while I committed my time and energy, as well as the costs of daily care and show expenses. We agreed that when the horse was sold, we would each recoup our investments and split any profit.

I found a 15.1-hand chestnut Thoroughbred (gelding, this time!) who I renamed Huckleberry Finn. He'd had a short racing career and been in his post-track home for just a few months, learning the basics of flatwork and "baby jumping" before I picked him up for $4,000. At the time, I didn't realize I was buying a horse for his temperament, but I definitely learned that was the case with Finn in the long run. I called him "small but mighty," because his heart was bigger than his natural athleticism would ever be. I've never had a horse try so hard for me as Finn did.

Finn was an absolute basket case at our first Beginner Novice event, as the atmosphere of a big show proved to be a huge trigger for him. I "rode through it," never feeling truly unsafe, and after that weekend, he began to get settled into the rhythm of competition:

travel, flat ride, sleep, dressage, jump, sleep, jump again, travel home, repeat. Over the course of two years, Finn turned into a tried-and-true Preliminary packer. He became the horse who could go anywhere, settle in, and do his job without batting an eye. For sure he had his quirks: he was terrified of pinto-colored horses—if they came toward him in the warm-up, he would spin and try to leave—but he got to where I could basically ride him around the cross country-phase on a loose rein, sitting up to let him know a jump was coming, and then softening to let him find it. He was correct in his dressage training, so he always scored well, even if he wasn't fancy, and he was careful, even if a bit quick, in the show jumping. When he had a hard time with a question I asked him along the way, he never hesitated to try again.

With all I know now, I can look back and say I'm sure my tack didn't fit Finn all that well, and he probably had ulcers, like ninety percent of his equine brethren…but he still would come running in from the field when I called him and try his heart out every day. As a trainer who thought she knew way more than she actually did, he was an absolute blessing.

I eventually sold Finn to a young rider in Texas, as I didn't believe he would be an Intermediate horse. I was dismayed to learn that not long after she got him, he pulled a suspensory ligament in turnout. I don't know that she ever got to compete with him, which broke my heart more than selling him did, as I knew he would be as much of a pleasure for his next rider as he had been for me.

After Finn, there was Lady Lucy. I'd helped Caroline find her, and she was meant to be Caroline's first "fancy" dressage horse. She came to me through Darren Chiacchia, who had gotten her from Chester Weber, a many-time international combined driving champion who also lived in Ocala. Lucy had been slated to be one of Chester's four-in-hand team, but she didn't grow to be as big as the other three horses, so she was sold as a riding horse instead.

Lucy was the perfect example of a horse with athletic talent to spare, but very little heart. We called her "Lucifer" in the barn—albeit with true affection. She had huge amounts of character and so much class and pizazz, but when you rode her, she didn't feel like she wanted to do the jobs she was being asked to do. There was a slight "No, thank you" in her at all times. When she was adrenalized, riding her could feel like floating on air. But it was next to impossible to elicit that feeling in her through training technique alone.

Lucy ended up being my ride as an event horse, rather than Caroline's ride as a dressage horse, because at random times, she could be a bit too "spicy" for an adult amateur. She usually did what I asked her to do, but I always got that sense she'd rather be somewhere else.

The contrast between the two Abingdon horses left me with an invaluable understanding: never underestimate *heart* and *try*, in horses or humans. To me, those two attributes are worth just as much as, *if not more than*, athleticism, good looks, and talent. A horse or a person can be gifted, gorgeous, and a born athlete, but if he doesn't want to pursue the thing you think he is suited for, you can't make him want it. A horse with *heart* and *try* will seek the harmony of partnership with his rider and jump through fire if you ask him to.

I would take ten Finns over one Lucy any day. He and his big-hearted brothers and sisters are the kind of horses that everyone needs in their life. I have also found that part of a horse having that kind of heart is usually also having the mind to back it up. There is an inquisitiveness and a willingness to play new games and try new things that comes linked with a heart that big. Now, when I look for a horse for myself or for clients, I prioritize these qualities. I look for horses who seek to understand the questions they are being asked—for the ones who don't quit or overreact when they don't comprehend, but who instead put on their thinking caps and look to me for more information. I'd rather have a horse who tries too hard and gives me a dozen wrong answers than a horse who tries one answer and then gives up or looks for the exit door.

The same goes for the humans. A person with a big heart and the willingness to be self-reflective (like I discussed in the last chapter), as well as to be vulnerable and to examine their own mind is someone I want to spend time with, even if that individual makes mistakes along the way. Of course, if talent and good looks come along with the rest of that package, then great. But when talent and good looks are all you rely on to get what you want in life, at some point, your looks will fade or your talent won't stack up in comparison to others, and you will fall short. In a relationship, when asked a hard question, you won't be willing to try and find the answer. You will opt for the easier route, because you are afraid of wading into murky water where you don't know what the outcome will be.

Sometimes the harder route is the better route, but it is impossible to do the harder things without a willing partner. This holds true for both horses and humans.

And then...there was Nick.

It wasn't long after Patrick and I separated that I started thinking about dating again. As I've shared, I was used to having a significant other in my life at all times. I missed that comfort and felt incredibly anxious about the prospect of being alone. I was not out looking for another husband, given my career priorities at that time (along with the fact that my divorce was not even final), but I did want to be in a committed relationship.

Nick and I met on match.com when online dating was just becoming a "thing." With my farm and competition schedule, I didn't have much time to go meet men out in the "real world," and I had definitely noticed there weren't many eligible bachelors at horse shows! All the men who were involved with horses seemed to be spoken for, in one way or another.

Nick was then a graduate student at Virginia Tech. He knew about "horse girls," as he happened to be dating one when he and I met. I learned, as we got to know each other through AOL instant messaging, that he had even taught at the Millbrook School, a private school that was affiliated with the long-held Millbrook Horse Trials in Millbrook, New York, a place I had frequented my whole young life. He also had a sister who lived in the town in which I had grown up in Connecticut.

There were so many interesting connections between us—we fell for each other, hard and fast. In the early days of our relationship, Nick would help me with barn chores on the weekends and drive for hours to watch me at competitions. I went on a lot of hikes and tried to take up disc golf to impress him. (That hobby was short-lived.) We had our fair share of ups and downs in that first year together—I was still reeling from my divorce, wondering if I really *did* want to be with someone or if I should spend some time alone, even though that was a very uncomfortable proposition for me, and Nick was still involved with another person, long-distance. At the same time, I truly felt like Nick was someone unusual and special in my life, and I didn't know that another would come along again if I let him go.

Our hearts kept pointing us back toward each other, so we kept taking next steps in our independent lives, while moving in the same general direction.

13
FINDING RESISTANCE

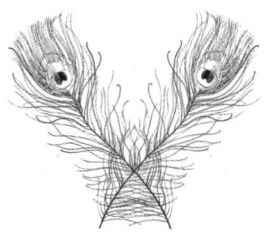

MY MOTHER ONCE SAID TO ME, "There will always be somebody better than you."

I don't remember the exact context of the statement, and I know now, looking back, that it was most likely meant to shore me up when I was down about my own performance. She was trying to build the understanding that there would be some things in life that I might be *really good* at, where I would maybe be better than the other people around me—but then there would be other things that I *wouldn't* be as good at, and in those moments, there would be other people better than me.

Somehow, though, my young mind internalized my mother's well-intended message as, "You will never be good enough; others will always be better."

This created a level of internal pressure I didn't realize I was putting on myself, despite what I had undeniably achieved with horses and the pats on the back I'd received from individuals I respected. *It wasn't enough.* I wanted to be seen as one of the best and accepted into what I perceived as a circle of greatness consisting of the upper-level riders I was competing against at eventing competitions.

For several years, I competed Finn, Lucy, and a handful of client horses every other weekend, riding against the likes of Boyd Martin, Buck Davidson, Doug Payne, Will Coleman, and Karen and David O'Connor. I *longed* to be noticed by them. I daydreamed about being picked out as special and seen as talented, as one deserving to be in their midst. The desperation I felt in those days is still palpable to me. I would be stabled down the aisle from one of the stars I was striving to be, and I would shyly say hello, hoping my introduction would lead to some deeper interaction, which it never did. I would go to the competitor parties often held on Saturday nights at events, and pray that one of the "top riders" would notice me, remember me, and ask me to join their elite table. I was surrounded by people constantly, all enjoying the sport I loved, but it was one of the loneliest times of my life. I was never happy. I was never satisfied with the success I had. What I experienced was never enough because I thought *I* was never going to be enough. I told myself I would only know I had "made it" if one of the riders I had put on a pedestal told me that I had.

During this time I was also teaching lessons for members of the local Pony Club. At one point, the District Commissioner of the Club put together a clinic with a woman who was working as a trainer under the O'Connors. I rode Lucy, and many of the younger Pony Club riders also attended. There was a teenage boy who had recently purchased a lovely, well-trained Thoroughbred to compete. The clinician took a liking to both this horse and the young rider, and at the end of the clinic, she offered him the opportunity to go and train at the O'Connors' for a couple of months that coming summer. I am embarrassed to admit that not only was I annoyed that one of my regular students, part of my relied-upon income, would be gone for a long chunk of time (therefore not paying me for lessons), but I was also incredibly jealous of the opportunity he had been offered. Someone had noticed his talent and wanted to help him develop it—he was being given what I had been wishing would happen for myself *for years*.

By that point I had a long-running internal story that told me I was always being held back because I could never afford a nice enough horse to be truly competitive. And from time to time, in moments like the one with the O'Connors' trainer, this narrative reared its ugly head. I was sure that if I had only been given the same opportunities other young riders who had moved up the ranks had, I would have "made it" already. Now, I began telling myself, I was simply too old to be singled out in such a way. For me, I was sure, *the opportunity was gone*. The whole situation with this clinician choosing a younger Pony Club member over me served to solidify my belief that I was on the "outside"—I was never going to make it and never going to be good enough.

In the grips of that story, I could not find a way to be happy for anyone who received the opportunities that I so deeply wanted. I was in a vicious cycle of jealousy, isolation, and false bravado, leading nowhere useful. I could only feel sorry for myself. The chip on my shoulder grew along with my neediness, and I'm sure it was palpable from the outside. Today, I can definitely sense it in others within whom I recognize my old tendencies. It is not an attractive quality. And it does not make you want to go out of your way to help or befriend that person.

I look back now, and I can see so many missed opportunities, like the opportunity to learn from and connect with other human beings in a genuine way, and the opportunity to truly appreciate what horses do for people and how our love for them connects us. I was so desperate to be part of some imagined elite club whose approval I was sure would mean I was "good enough" and that I would "make it" that I wasn't open to other possibilities or directions. I thought that riding at the Olympic level was the *only* end game that meant anything because it would prove that I was better than all the other riders who never reached that level. But instead of honing the skills I had and feeling grateful for the horses I could ride, I spent all my time thinking about the things I *didn't* have. I lived in a state of *lack*. A scarcity mindset. I thought that working harder and pushing through would improve the situation I perceived to be so poor, but all it did was lead to burnout. I was exhausted and frustrated and couldn't see the gift that was the horses who were right in front of me. I could not see the opportunity these "imperfect" beings afforded me to learn and understand others in different ways. As a rider, and as a human, I wasn't ready for that lesson yet. I had to sink lower, hit my rock bottom, before I could figure out a new way to be with myself, with other people, and perhaps most importantly, with horses.

I was in my early twenties when my life and my negative mindset started to feel unsustainable as it was. There was no joy. All I did was drive relentlessly toward a seemingly unattainable goal—one that I had voiced out loud to so many people in my life that turning back from it felt like it would be just another failure, like my recent divorce. I didn't know what to do or which way to turn. All I knew was that I was *unhappy* in my life with horses, and for so long, horses had been my saving grace and place of peace.

Sometimes, when the path you are on feels like a one-way ride, you can't even imagine that other paths might exist. So you soldier on, with blinders in place, and you wonder what the point of each day's struggle toward a goal is when you're never going to be good enough to reach it.

Looking back, it's tempting to see that chunk of my twenties as a waste of time and energy, and to kick myself for all the missed opportunities and for what I can see was a lot of wallowing in self-pity. But that period was part of my path. We all have hills and valleys we need to walk over and through. It's cliche, I know, but they are what shape us. They apply the necessary pressure to create change. Without discomfort from a struggle up or a fall down, there's no real impetus to step in a different direction.

I think there are four quadrants that people and horses fit into when it comes to relating to pressure and change:

- The first people and horses have a *high tolerance for discomfort* and resist change, even though another choice or path might make them happier. They might be called "stubborn" or "close-minded." I fell into this quadrant.

- The next people and horses have almost *no tolerance for discomfort*, and yet they still resist change. They, however, do so out of fear of what might happen when they try something new. They get stuck easily, but they don't seek another path, so anxiety and frustration grow as they circle the same endless drain.

- Then there are those people and horses with a *low tolerance for discomfort* and a high desire for change. They look for the path of least resistance. They may end up taking a path that's easier because it feels safe and non-threatening, but they may never realize their full potential because they are too afraid to fail.

Lastly, there are those with a *high tolerance for discomfort* and a high desire for change. They don't mind a bit of pressure. They know that all good things come with some discomfort, but they don't fight growth. They seek it. They want to understand things in different ways, even when it feels like a harder path than the other options in front of them. They know what lies at the other end might just be worth it.

14
FINDING THE BOTTOM

I COULD FEEL her resistance right out of the start box, from the very beginning of the course. Lucy was very much behind the leg, but at the time, I thought it was simply how she went around cross-country courses. I knew she was not as hot as the Thoroughbreds I had mostly ridden up to that point. I thought that she had simply settled out of her green "spiciness" into a horse with a big stride but not much desire to go. After all, we had done a brief stint at Beginner Novice, and she'd won almost every event we entered. We had done our due diligence at Novice level with similar results. It was time to move up. That was how it worked. That's what came next.

What I didn't understand was that Lucy was unsure of the harder questions I was now asking her. I was more worried about making time than I was thoughtful about how I presented the jumps. I headed into the woods, riding hard toward the first water obstacle, which began with a brush fence.

I didn't expect the brush to be something Lucy looked at, but as we approached, she was fixated on the shadowy water just beyond, and she barely registered the jump in front of her. Lucy lost momentum, I kicked and used my stick, and she clambered over it. I felt her left shoulder drop out from under me as her front end only half-cleared the brush, and we went down. I fell toward the left, my leg under Lucy as she rolled on top of me.

It all happened in such slow motion that she and I were still in basically the same place, just on the other side of the jump, as we both climbed to our feet. My mind, though, was now in fast-forward: *How many penalty points will this cost me? Will it knock me out of the ribbons? Is there any way I can still make time? How many people are watching? What do they think of my riding? What will Caroline say when I tell her? What will Nick and my friends and family say?*

Back in those days, you could have a fall on a cross-country course, get back on, and keep going. Technically, we had gotten through the flags at the brush. Lucy's well-being didn't even enter my stream of rapid-fire thoughts as I climbed up and rode through the water, kicking her to continue on.

Somehow, we finished the course. I literally have no recollection of the rest of the jumps; I just remember how backward Lucy felt, like I had to force her over every obstacle.

As we walked back to the barn and the adrenaline left my body, I realized that my left ankle felt stiff and swollen inside my boot. I took care of Lucy, worried about whether I would even be able to pull my left boot off. Luckily, when I did, I found that the ankle didn't appear to be broken, only badly sprained. I limped around, packing to head home. I barely looked up as I moved, sure that everyone at the show was judging me. I was convinced they knew I was the girl who'd fallen over the brush at the water, gotten back on, and made her horse keep going. By then, the guilt about how I had treated Lucy was settling in, alongside the swelling in my ankle and overwhelming embarrassment.

Lucy would barely look at me. I didn't have the understanding of what had happened back then, but I now know that the trust between us was gone, and that I had broken it. The guilt I feel about that now is still devastating.

It took me twice as long as usual to pack and load my rig because of my ankle, and by the time I got on the road for home, I was more physically and emotionally exhausted than I had ever been in my life. I had moved on from embarrassment and guilt to berating myself endlessly for my stupidity and terrible riding. I had found my rock bottom. I kept thinking, *I will never amount to anything in the competitive world. I am just another rider. I am not a winner. I will never be someone that anyone will notice.*

I am worthless.

And then, it was like someone grabbed me by the shoulders and shook me. My eyes opened wide with the realization of what I was doing, and the shock of it made me gasp. In a flash I recognized that I was equating my value as a human being with the outcome of that show. I had set my worthlessness in stone, based on my placing at one event. I could not decipher the difference between a bad decision I had made for my horse and my merit as a person in the world.

At that moment I also realized I had been doing this for a very, very long time, and I saw how unbelievably unhealthy it was—how unsustainable and how unsatisfying my life would be if I continued in this way. I knew, within a two-minute span of sudden and startling clarity, that I had to make some drastic changes if I ever wanted to enjoy my life and the horses in it.

For the first time ever, I acknowledged that a person was more than the sum of wins minus losses. I know now that when your self-worth is firmly attached to the idea of "making it," you will never be content with anything in this life. And from the outside, if we judge others by their worldly "success," we may be missing the opportunity to connect with them in a truly genuine way. The people and horses I love and admire most in this world will likely never be in the limelight for having won anything, but their presence is a gift to everyone they touch. I try to make sure they know.

I downplayed the fall with Lucy as bad luck, telling people who weren't at the event that her bell boot got caught on the brush of the jump, and leaving out the unseemly details of how it actually all unfolded. I had a long-time habit of retelling the stories of my life in ways I thought would make me more likable and make me seem like less of a failure. At the same time, my realizations on the drive back meant I knew it was a habit I needed to change if I was ever going to actually believe that my value as a person and my performance in the competitive world were not inextricably linked. I just had no idea how to change that belief or that habit.

So, I began searching. I was asking myself existential questions about the meaning of life and the point of a human existence. I Googled questions like "What is self?" and "What is ego?" I was directed to mostly links to Buddhist teachings and Eastern philosophical ideas, and while reading one of the articles, I remembered a book that had been sitting on my bookshelf, unread, for many years, having been a gift from a relative when I was in college. The book was *The Art of Happiness* by the Dalai Lama. I devoured that book, and others like it, in the weeks and months to come, reading and rereading passages, and reeling with new ideas that somehow already resonated with me on a deep level and seemed to apply directly to me personally. I felt like I was uncovering truths that I had already known, somewhere in my being, but had forsaken in my efforts to "become someone." I knew I had to go deeper into understanding those truths, and in doing so, understanding myself. I knew this was the only way I could truly love my life with horses again.

One of the things that the books emphasized was the importance of having a *teacher*. Simply put, this *teacher* was a personal guide on the path to understanding the nature of being. It was someone to point you in the right direction when you had questions or came upon a fork in the road and didn't know which way to turn. I felt drawn to this idea, as I already had questions that weren't easily answered by the books I was reading, and I yearned for more support on my journey. I'd had a riding instructor almost my whole life, so it was a familiar and comforting idea. I also knew somewhere deep down that without a guide, I would most likely fall back into old habits and patterns. I needed someone to keep me honest.

So I set out to find a teacher, preferably one I could work with in person. The idea of going on a meditation retreat interested me. I had been trying to meditate on my own at home, using books as my guides, with what felt like very limited success. I thought that immersing myself in guided meditation practice for several days might both help answer some immediate questions and connect me with a long-term teacher. I found a retreat center within an hour of Caroline's farm, just outside of Charlottesville, Virginia, and they just so happened to be holding a Tibetan yoga retreat the weekend of my twenty-seventh birthday. I signed up with both excitement and trepidation. The same insecurities that plagued me in all social situations were following me into the meditation world: *Will people like me? Will I be good at meditating? Will others be able to tell when I'm not getting it? Will I look weird doing it? Will everyone there be a better meditator than me?*

That first retreat, I spent much of my time wondering if I was doing things right and feeling silly, but I dove in nonetheless, attending and participating in every practice session, and spending time meditating on my own outside the group gatherings—probably more out of my desire to be seen as a "star pupil" than out of any real understanding. But my tenacity served me well that weekend, even if it was misguided. I started to feel like everything and everyone around me was more alive, more fresh, more clear. It felt like I was living in a dream state where everything was more vivid than in the "real world." What surprised me the most, though, was that when the retreat was over, and I went into Charlottesville with some new friends I had made over the weekend, the vividness continued: The colors around me were brighter, the trees more full of life in the wind; the ice cream we got tasted better than any I had ever eaten before; the people we talked to seemed friendlier and more open to connection.

Then, it struck me. I wasn't living in a dream at that moment. I had finally *woken up* out of one. I was truly present in the moment for probably the first time in over twenty years.

I had just barely begun clearing away the fog and debris that had been obscuring my natural state of being, which as it turned out was open, warm, and confident. The difference was so stark, I felt like someone had just turned on a spotlight in a room that had been dark for centuries. I did not want to go back into the dark, and I was terrified I wouldn't be able to turn the light on again. As I made my way home, panic began to set in: *What if I never feel this way again?*

What if the only way to feel this way is to live as a Buddhist after giving away all my worldly possessions and moving to Tibet? What if I have to give up horses and my riding goals to feel this way?

Poor Nick. He had asked me to marry him just prior to my quarter-life crisis, and when I got home from the retreat, he genuinely wondered if I had joined a cult. Looking back, I can understand why he was concerned. I basically told him that the five days in Charlottesville had completely changed the way I saw the world and that I didn't know if I could ever go back to the way things had been prior to it. In my mind, that meant my life with horses, and possibly my planned life with Nick, needed to change. It was a very messy and frightening time for both of us. I felt guilty for hurting him, and at the same time, so sure that I had to make major shifts in my life if I was ever going to feel fulfilled. I had a sense that if I was going to be able to look back at my life and feel like I had done something worthwhile, I had to start following a very different path than the one I had been traveling up to that point, and I didn't know who or what that included. I only knew that something had to give, in a major way.

I tried to keep competing like I always had, because I had to make a living. I had started working for Caroline full-time, running her private facility and riding her lovely horses. I knew I was "living the dream" of so many working equestrians, and I was trying to make it work. I strung up a little set of paper Tibetan prayer flags in my truck to remind me of that feeling I'd had on retreat, but my foray into the meditation world was so short in comparison to the years of self-deprecating habits. I fell back into familiar patterns of berating myself, this time for not doing a better job of becoming a better person. I put on a façade of equanimity and serenity, but the same fears and desperations still plagued me. I knew I had only scratched the surface of a deeper understanding that could truly shift the way I moved through my life. but the level of change I was contemplating felt like the most daunting thing I had ever considered. It meant upending every aspect of my life. It seemed like I would have to give up on my dreams, tell the world I was choosing to give up on them, and then be judged by all for the choice.

But I couldn't *unsee* what I had experienced at that retreat. I couldn't *unfeel* that sense of lightness and ease. I wanted to be able to do the things I loved with horses, and have that sense of wholeness I'd so briefly felt while I did it. It seemed like it had to be possible, but what if I let go of everything I had worked to achieve, and it wasn't? I knew I wasn't willing to go on living the way I had been, and if I was ever going to feel like my life had joy and meaning and that I had inherent value, I had to take that leap. I was still that person with a high tolerance for discomfort, and I was becoming a person who also had a high desire for change.

Sometimes you have to start from scratch, take a look at the foundation, and repair that before you start building again. I had long hoped I could just use some duct tape and bailing twine and shore things up as I went, but as I had learned the hard way with Lucy, that wasn't a great plan. Patches wouldn't hold forever. If there were holes in the foundation, eventually the building would crumble. Now that I had experienced what it felt like to be whole and stable, even for a brief time, the patches I had used all the years prior were just an ugly reminder that things within me were not as they should be.

Often people get very impatient when I tell them their horses need to go back to groundwork. They want to keep on doing what they have been doing, even though they have come to me because the things they are doing aren't working. They want to slap on patches rather than take the time to fix the foundation. Having gone through the foundation-repair process on myself, I am completely unwilling to do it any other way with horses. If you want a quick fix for yourself or your horse, I'm not your girl. I want to strip it all back down to the studs, start building slowly, stop whenever necessary to assess and redesign, and take my time to appreciate what starts to take shape. I want to enjoy the process, not just the end result. I want to notice those little moments of understanding in myself, the people around me, and the horses I work with. I want to take the time to celebrate them, and then I want to look back continually, and notice how far we've come. I want to appreciate and have gratitude for the accumulation of small changes that led to something I could never have imagined.

This is where I find true joy in working with horses.

15
FINDING SOFTNESS

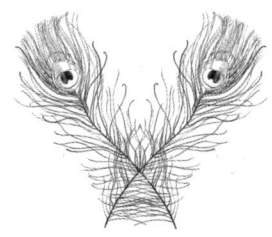

WE CALLED OFF THE WEDDING.

We lost our deposits on the ceremony and reception sites. I had to call my family and friends and tell them that the "save the date" cards we had sent could be tossed in the recycling bin. And I had to hope that Nick would be willing to take a different path with me and be patient while I bushwhacked my way through the mess I was currently stuck in.

I had to tell Caroline, my closest friend during my years in Virginia, that I was leaving the role of running her farm—a multimillion-dollar private facility with a small number of nice horses that Caroline allowed me to show and ride, and a job that anyone in my profession would have died for. *What the hell am I thinking?* I asked myself that question over and over again. But I also asked myself if I would be satisfied with my life if managing Caroline's farm was what I did for the next twenty years. It looked so good on paper!

I hated that the answer was no.

Nick's mom, Louise, was very sick with multiple myeloma, a type of bone cancer with limited treatment options at that time. It was really important to him that we move to Maine where he could be close to his family while his mother was still alive. Somewhere in my search for meaning, I came up with the idea that doing so, as Nick wished, and then stepping into social service might leave me feeling like I had led a life worth living when all was said and done. I thought it might mean more if, instead of supporting a hobby popular with the elite of the world, I got my hands dirty in a different way, trying to help my fellow man.

Nick and I packed our lives and our large number of pets into a moving truck and my three-horse, slant-load trailer, and headed for Maine. I didn't have a job yet. We had a house to rent that allowed our pets, which was very hard to find and very expensive. We couldn't actually afford it, but we took the leap regardless.

The first three months were strange and difficult. Nick had to go back to Virginia after we had settled in, as he had to finish up a few things for this graduate degree. I was left alone in a whole new state…and it wouldn't stop snowing. I didn't have a job or friends in the area, and I had sworn off horses for a while because I was burnt out and needed a break from my relationship with them. I wanted to be a better person. A healthier person. A happier person.

When we came up on our second month of rent, we were short. I didn't know what I was going to do, as I was supposed to be the one writing the check. I was interviewing for jobs and felt hopeful about one in particular, but no paychecks were forthcoming for the time being. I had drained my savings. I did not want to ask my parents for money.

Just before rent was due, I went out to the mailbox and found a small envelope labeled with my name and an address in Laurel Bloomery, Tennessee. It was from Marilyn Mitchell. When I opened it, to my complete shock, I found a check for $2,000! I could not believe what I was looking at. There was also a handwritten note, explaining that Marilyn felt she had been unfair in the commission she had given me on a couple of horses we had sold together. She wanted to make it right by sending me what she thought she owed me.

To this day, I cannot believe the miracle of that check's arrival in our mailbox. I don't even know how she found my rental address!

It was fitting that Marilyn was the first person who had shared with me the idea that the universe will provide what you need...*if you are open to the possibility of receiving it.* I could see the parallel between this "new age" idea of manifesting, popularized in a book at that time called *The Secret* by Rhonda Byrne, and the teachings of the Buddhist tradition I had begun to follow. I was learning about the idea that each of us is "whole and complete" as we are, in every moment, and that in turning toward the "shared space of being" that all sentient beings inhabit, we find that everything we need in life is available to us. I don't think my Buddhist teacher necessarily meant that a check would show up in the mail just when I needed it, but I do think he was pointing me toward having a calm and open sense that things will work out in a way that I have the tools to navigate through. This could mean any myriad of outcomes to any given situation—it was more about achieving an attitude of *openness to possibility* than about expecting things to work out in my favor in an easily predicted way. I needed to learn to let things unfold, rather than panicking about the unknown end results.

I got the job I was hoping to get at a group home called Mary's Place. It was a safe space for young women and their children, where the "moms" were diagnosed with co-occurring mental health and substance use disorders. I had zero experience in social service, but the supervisor at the home, Amanda, gave me a shot. She could tell I was no stranger to hard work, that I was a highly organized person, and that I had a desire to learn. In some ways, even as someone new to the field, working at Mary's Place was far easier, at first, than working with horses. There was very little pressure related to performance. There was no goal to be attained or accolade to win. There were just people navigating life and its daily ups and downs. Don't get me wrong, anyone who has ever worked in social service can tell you that helping individuals with extensive trauma histories and limited coping skills is exhausting in its own way, and when you add young children to the mix, the emotional turmoil can be incredibly taxing. *But it wasn't about me.* I didn't have to prove myself at Mary's Place in the way I felt I had to in the horse world.

Interestingly, I could also see strong parallels between my work with horses and my work with the women and their children, which helped me tremendously as I stepped into the social work world. For example, *boundaries were paramount* at Mary's Place. They created safety for both staff and residents, even when they were sometimes difficult to enforce. The women didn't know they needed rules to follow, but once they understood them, they could more easily settle into relationships with staff and each other. This, in turn, actually allowed them to relax and be themselves without fear of accidentally making a mistake or getting in trouble. And once the mothers at Mary's Place understood what it felt like to have boundaries held in place for themselves, they could begin holding boundaries for their children, which kept everyone safer. Boundaries with horses are the same—they keep everyone safe and create a structure that allows for relaxation and self-expression because everyone knows what the limits are. Everything inside those limits is fair game, and that way there are no surprises. With both the humans at Mary's Place and horses, the boundaries had to be reinforced often, with patience and consistency, before they could be considered truly *learned*.

A big part of the riding instructor's job is listening to clients. Sometimes you get to hear funny or interesting stories about their lives outside the farm and you commiserate over shared experiences. Sometimes you listen to their problems, because it's clear in the way they are relating to their horses that they are not fully present on a given day, and talking about what's going on is the only way to move productively forward. You can't force someone to tell you about their difficulties, but you can leave the door open so they know they can. More than once, for the sake of the horse, I have needed to redirect a rider to a simpler exercise because that person simply isn't able to be present enough to work with the horse on the original plan. In that scenario, I will ask, "Is everything okay?" I may get a short, curt affirmative reply, or I may get instant tears and outpouring of a story. I'm there for either, holding space for whatever is needed in that moment, and making sure everyone stays physically safe through the process. All my years of teaching riding lessons with this mentality had prepared me for similar aspects of the job at Mary's Place.

I made it three months, cold-turkey zero-contact, before I had to get my hands on a horse. My job had begun to feel emotionally draining, and I again sought safety and comfort in the animals I loved so much. I found a local barn where I could catch-ride some ponies that needed to be sold. It was a hunter barn, which was quite a different environment for me. There were some standard practices and beliefs about training that I very much disagreed with, but that were commonplace at this facility, so I kept my head down and did the best work I knew how to do. I found that because I wasn't depending on my work with horses to earn a living, there was a newfound freedom to be patient and take my time with them. I found myself listening more closely to feedback the horses were giving me during training sessions. I was quicker to notice a "softening" or a "give" in the horse, and to respond in kind. The sale ponies I was working with improved quickly, and other people at the barn began to notice.

Sometimes you think you are going to "make a difference" and you end up learning a lot more about yourself than you end up helping others. This was the case for me when I stepped into social service. I thought I was doing a "greater good" than I was in the horse world. But I found that people were harder to influence than horses. They tended to have a lot more baggage and to be more resistant to change. They fell back into old habits more easily than horses, even when presented with simpler options. Perhaps I had always known this, and that was why I had preferred training horses over teaching people to ride, but it was reinforced for me in my work at Mary's Place.

It was also reinforced that you never know what small thing you might say or do that will have an effect on someone's life that you may never know about. Sometimes staff would hear messages of thanks from the women who had been residents of Mary's Place months, or even years, after they'd left the program. Often the women thanking the staff had moved on in less-than-ideal circumstances, and we worried for their and their children's safety. But they had to run into a level of pressure that required change and make that choice themselves. I and the others at Mary's Place couldn't make it happen for them. We could only point in the direction of less resistance and encourage the young mothers to try something new.

I applied the awareness I was acquiring as I navigated pressure and choice with the families at Mary's Place with the horses I was helping with at the hunter barn. I was learning to suggest things and then wait for the horses to process their choices. The process made me wonder if there was a better way to help humans and horses—a way that could create more lasting and authentic change.

During this time, Nick and I replanned our wedding, which took place in June of 2009. We made it a much smaller affair in Acadia National Park—it poured buckets and was still beautiful. It felt much more authentic than what we had originally planned. As we honeymooned on a road trip to Nova Scotia, we started talking about when we would have kids. I didn't know if or when I would ever step back into a full-time career with horses. I was almost thirty years old and felt my biological clock ticking. I was learning a ton about parenting and child brain development at Mary's Place, and it seemed like the right time to try and have a family.

In February of 2011, our daughter Graesyn was born. I had never been so determined to do something right as I was with parenting that child. Turns out there's just as much folly in attempting parenting perfection as there is in attempting riding perfection. I learned the hard way that turning parenting into a goal-oriented competition with oneself or the other moms around you is a recipe for unhappiness in the same way it is with horses. And of course parenting children and training horses have a lot of parallels, *patience* and *consistency* being two of the most obvious. The biggest difference is that the upset of your child will always be harder to manage than the upset of a horse.

It just tugs at your heartstrings in a different way, which I couldn't fully understand until I had my own child.

I had been traveling down to Virginia every December between Christmas and New Year's for the annual winter retreat at the same meditation center outside Charlottesville. Nick had come with me once, just to make sure I wasn't *really* joining a cult, but the experience was not for him, so I had continued to go on my own. I did my best to keep up a personal practice in between retreats—much easier said than done when you're first learning to meditate and parenting your first child.

At Mary's Place I was learning a lot about different techniques and interventions such as *cognitive and dialectic behavior therapy* and *motivational interviewing*, which were clearly rooted in mindfulness practices. I was also taking a deep dive into advances in neuroscience that pertained to early child development that also gave credit to long-held understandings of Buddhist cultures and Eastern philosophies. It felt like the main avenues of my life were running parallel, except for the part that included horses. My time with them didn't feel like the stress-inducing dilemma I had left in Virginia, but was instead more like it had been when I was younger—a respite from the *other* stresses of my life. I was grateful for this change, but I had a sense that at some point, in some bigger way, the horses would join the flow I now had going in other areas. I longed for this and knew I just had to stay open to how it would happen.

The first of many gray horses in my life, Smokey (left) was my door to the feelings of freedom and flow that horses can bring. (My grandfather took me to the races in Saratoga Springs, New York, a few times as a child, and said I always wanted him to bet on grays!) Brewster (below) was my first "heart horse." I wish every one of my students could have a horse like him in their life.

Photo left by Nicholas Auclair; below by Joy Auclair

Pony Club provided connections that ensured I had horses to ride throughout my youth, like Gator (right). Mikey (below) proved to be a more athletic partner than I could have imagined when I found his "for sale" ad in the newspaper.

Photo right and far right courtesy of Chelsea Canedy; below by Steve Milne

Though our time together was short, Gabby was one of the sweetest teachers I had the privilege to know.

Lucy (above) was the horse who helped me find my turning point. Blue (below) was the first horse I ever bought for myself. He and Eddie (right) taught me that you never have enough tools in your toolbox.

Photos above courtesy of Chelsea Canedy; right by Kim Beaudoin/KTB Creative

I chose to see working with Eddie as a learning opportunity.

Albert was my first "orange"—a horse with the athletic potential to excel at the higher levels of eventing.

Many found it unusual that I regularly worked my performance horses at liberty, in a rope halter, or brideless with just a neck ring, but I stuck to my values and what brought me joy, even when my techniques were questioned.

Photos courtesy of Noelle Floyd

Willow, my Boxer (and sidekick), and Albert were bright lights in the dark years of the pandemic.
Photo by Sally Spickard

I had to learn how to balance the "competitive me" who aspired to ride at the highest levels and be recognized for my achievements, with the joyful me who simply loved everything about being with horses. I am still working on mastering this balance today.

Photos by Kim Beaudoin/KTB Creative

Lila was my reset button, always relaxed and ready to learn new things.

Unexpected Farm, with its incredible historic round barn, became a reality only because of a perfectly aligned series of events. I am so grateful that the universe clicked into place to allow for this opportunity.

Photo right and far right by Kim Beaudoin/KTB Creative; below by Katie Liscovitz

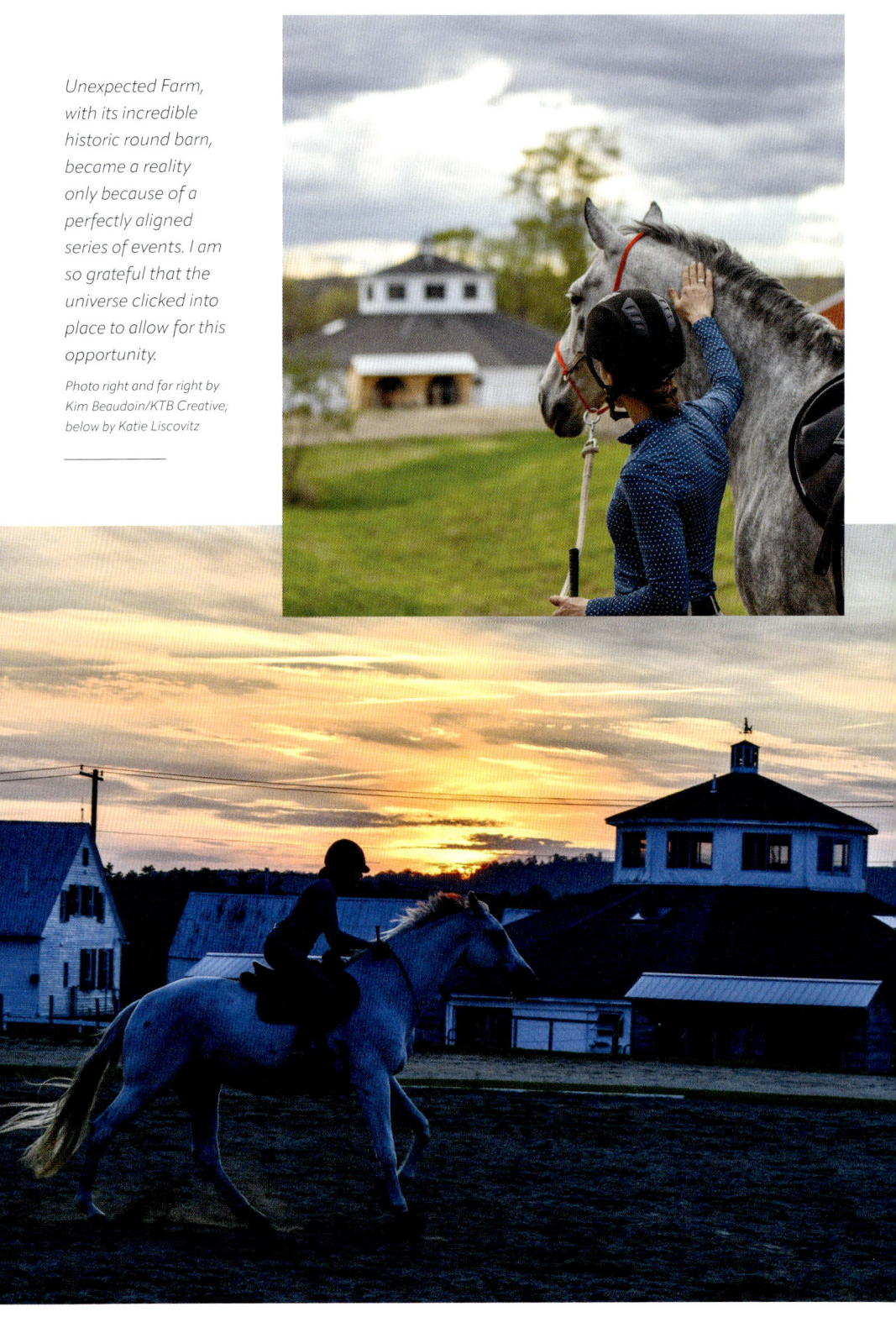

If I've learned anything in my years of studying horses and horsemanship, it is that no one way is the right way.

Luna, in all her Mustang ways, was so aware and "street smart." She taught me what it is like to really be true to yourself.

The Mustang Classic gave me a chance to showcase the correct horsemanship skills Luna and I had built in our time together. I was so proud of Luna's performance, and I will never tire of hugging her, for no other reason than it is her.

Photo far left by Ronda Gregorio; left by Katie Liscovitz; and below by Alicia Marie Photography

I am excited to see where my developing relationship with Fox, my most athletic partner to date, will take us!

Left photo by Jennifer Johnson; below by Hannah Marie Photography

16
FINDING TRANSFORMATION

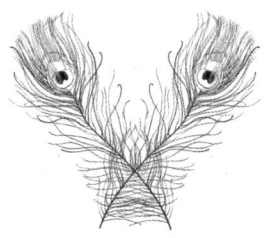

MY LONGTIME TEACHER, Tenzin Wangyal Rinpoche, had put together a new meditation program called The 3 Doors Academy, which took the essential teachings of the Tibetan Bon lineage that Rinpoche was descended from and boiled them down into a two-and-a-half-year, nonsecular, intensive self-reflection and meditation journey. I felt deeply in my heart that I needed to be part of the Academy, despite knowing I couldn't financially afford it, so I basically begged to be let in, pledging to do whatever work I needed to in order to make my presence valuable. It turned out they were looking for a retreat coordinator for the next session, and my familiarity with the teacher and location made me an ideal choice for the job. After coming to an agreement with the heads of the fledgling Academy, I was able to afford the tuition with my substantial work discount, and the next chapter of my self-discovery began.

Despite by then being a meditation practitioner for six years, I knew I had still barely scratched the surface of what I sought to uncover by exploring my inner landscape. I felt like I had been just playing at meditation, trying to fake it until I made it, but that there were some essential pieces I was missing. And I was right. I knew it on the first day of my first Academy retreat.

Though cathartic and at times incredibly therapeutic, The 3 Doors Academy was not therapy in any traditional sense. The lessons in that two-and-a-half years of my life were some of the most intense and uncomfortable I had ever experienced. It was a different kind of discomfort than I was used to: the kind that comes from looking at yourself and your long-standing habits in a way you have never done before; the kind that comes from befriending yourself and all of your idiosyncrasies in a way you didn't know was possible; the kind that comes from sitting in your shit rather than trying to avoid it, run past it, or escape from it.

The Academy group of thirty-five people met every six months for a week-long retreat and committed to a personal daily practice of at least forty-five minutes of meditation, intensive journaling, as well as "personal retreat days," without the guidance or support of the group or our usual teachers. It was a huge commitment for me to make, given our young family and my full-time job. Ahead of every single retreat, I would hem and haw about going at all, feeling that I could not possibly take the time away from all my responsibilities. To save money, I would drive to Virginia, either alone or carpooling with a fellow Academy participant. The drives were long and exhausting, about twelve hours each way. And at the end of every retreat, I would struggle with the idea of reintegrating into my normal daily life, having so fully immersed myself into retreat living and the rhythm of long meditations and group sharing. The movement between my two extremes was often jarring and difficult to manage, but it was all worth it.

I can honestly say that I came out on the other side of the Academy a completely different human than I went in.

I showed up at my first Academy retreat the exact same way I had showed up for Camp Laurel, the first days of high school and college, and every big horse show I ever entered—desperately seeking to fit in and be noticed as special and worthy of knowing. When I left the Academy, I could see those aspects of myself as separate from who I truly am. I could be kind to them, like I would a dear friend who was experiencing separateness and insecurity. I could allow those feelings to come and go without trying to get rid of them, hating them for existing, or hating myself for allowing them to appear again. I could see the destructive patterns of behavior in my life as learned habits rather than character flaws.

I attribute all these changes to having truly experienced myself and those around me as vast, open beings, capable of awareness, warmth, and love, and beyond what we thought ourselves capable of, through the practice of meditation. The people in the Academy with me became family. We will always share a bond that is indescribable, having borne witness to the transformations each of us underwent. The Academy became yet another space in my life where my experiences trumped what I could understand with my moving mind and usual powers of observation. It reminded me that *felt experience* is often more powerful and true than anything we can learn from a book or a video.

The lessons I learned during that time of my life are too numerous to recount, but they boil down to this:

| The voice in your head that you think is you is not.

| Your thoughts are no more solid than a wisp of a cloud in a clear blue sky. They feel solid and heavy because of the way

we build a story around them. Left alone without a story, they will dissolve and all you'll be left with is vast clarity and endless possibility.

> Your thoughts aren't the enemy or something to be fought with. They're more like the caw of a crow or the sound of an engine as it passes. They come and go. They can be disruptive, but in the end they are simply pointing you back to the open space from which they emerged.

None of this is to say that problems don't exist and aren't substantial. It is all to say that how we deal with those problems can be very different than we imagine. Do we react out of habit and fear or do we come from openness and warmth? Can we trust that everything will resolve, even if it's not in a way we thought it would? Can we be curious about all the possibilities? I am the first to acknowledge that I am nowhere near perfect at this. Many of my long-standing habits still exist, but I try to relate to them in a very different way now. To do this is a commitment and a constant practice, and one that I don't always manage well. But it's now the backdrop from which I try to move through my life. I can't unknow what I now know to be the truth of being, and it has shaped the way my life has unfolded since then.

17
FINDING MY OWN WAY
————

DURING THE YEARS I committed to the Academy, I also accumulated a small number of lesson and training clients. Several people had approached me at the hunter barn, asking if I would teach them, and I agreed. It turns out, when you do good work for the right reasons, people notice. Humans are drawn to genuineness, to authenticity, and to presence, because those are the feelings everyone wants for themselves. As creatures who live in the present moment (without even having to try), horses are attracted to the same things.

When I told the owner of the hunter barn about the interest I was hearing from the clients and that I planned to move to a different facility to teach them, she didn't begrudge me the income that she knew I desperately needed. I was grateful for her understanding, and soon had four to five full-time students, as well as my full-time job at Mary's Place.

During those years, even while I was balancing work with parenting a young daughter, there was always a little part of me looking for *the* horse that would put me on the "eventing map," though at that point, I couldn't tell if it was a real desire or just a habitual behavior. I relied on my strong personal meditation practice when I noticed my old troublesome patterns creeping in and was learning in real time that sometimes *what you think you want* and *what you need* are two very different things. I was still acquiring the ability to balance the hustle and the flow, the drive to succeed and the openness to possibilities. I was finding the joy in working with horses again, but had to keep it somewhere between determination and flexibility.

When I became pregnant with my second child, the small number of clients I had been helping dwindled. Horses I was deeply attached to were pulled from my program, and I took a few serious hits to my ego. Yet again, I was left questioning the idea of horses as a profession, which had been a possibility I was lightly entertaining, while also knowing I wanted to have a second child.

The night I got home from the group graduation from The 3 Doors Academy, I went into labor with my son, Finnegan. We had just gotten Graesyn into bed after our twelve-hour car ride home from Virgina, and we were unpacking the car when I bent down to put something away, and my water broke. My mom was called into action for Graesyn, and Nick and I left for the hospital in Portland, where Finn was born early the next morning. And the moment he came into the world, I knew two things: our family was now complete, and it was time to have a horse of my own. I felt the immediate need to take back that part of my life in a more substantial way.

Parenting two young children can be very monotonous and all-consuming, and as a person who'd always thrived on variety in life, I knew my mental health needed a boost. Young children are, by nature, very needy, and my son was more so than many at the beginning of his life. He was fussy and wanted to be constantly attached to me physically. Buying my own horse—just for me, not for a client or for resale—felt like a project that would give me some sense of independent direction and accomplishment, outside of raising our kids. I wanted something that was *just mine*—no more relying on riding other people's horses to pursue any of my personal goals or worrying that a ride on a horse I enjoyed would be taken from me. I honestly had no idea what my goals even were at that point, but I was tired of the heartache I felt when people gave the rides on their horses to other trainers.

During the first few weeks of Finn's life, I got a new tattoo. I had been planning it for a while, to honor my personal growth over the past few years: two peacock feathers, intertwined and winding their way up my left upper arm, ending with a flourish at my shoulder (peacock feathers are a symbol of transformation and awareness, and they represented my watchful eye over my children). I also spent any free time calling local farms to inquire about board costs and amenities. The pickings were slim with my budget, desired driving radius, and requirement for an indoor arena, paramount for riding through the winter in Maine. I visited a few and settled on Upper Pond Stables in Litchfield, Maine, as the place I would bring the horse I planned on buying for myself.

With a little more research, it became glaringly apparent that all I could afford was an off-the-track Thoroughbred, which often sold for very little when their racing careers were over and were also very common in the eventing world because of their energy and athleticism. So one afternoon, while Finn was napping and Graesyn was playing with her grandparents, I started looking at ads for Thoroughbreds and found a handsome bay gelding called In DeBlue, who had just retired from the track in Massachusetts. I didn't hesitate. The price was right, so I made the call to schedule a time to go and see him.

Blue seemed sound and sane enough, so, somewhat impulsively, I signed the sales agreement, paid his owner, and brought him to Upper Pond that very day. It was like something out of a dream. I had literally never chosen my own horse up to that point. I had ridden other people's horses and had sales projects that involved others' investments, but I had never had a horse that was just for me for the long-term. I wasn't in any particular hurry and had no specific goals for Blue, other than he was a horse for me to enjoy, teach, and learn from. I was in total shock…and also in heaven.

My first year with Blue was relatively easy. There were certainly some habits and behaviors he had that challenged me, but nothing overly so. He progressed in what I would have called a "normal" fashion. His flatwork came along as well as his tight Thoroughbred body would allow, and he slowly began to understand the basic ideas of leg aids and contact. I found that he wasn't overly anxious about learning to jump, as I taught him how to navigate trot rails, then cross-rails, then small jumps, and then obstacles with fill underneath them. He had his more rambunctious moments, and I tried to integrate the groundwork I knew when they arose. Since Blue was mine, and I didn't care what the other people at Upper Pond thought about what I was doing, I felt confident with my rope halter and the tools that Marilyn had imparted upon me years prior. My long-time trainer Steve started coming to the East Coast to teach on a monthly basis, and I got his help whenever he was in town. I was a student again, and I loved it. I loved it even when the only time I could get to the barn was after I put Finn to bed at night, arriving there around 7:30 pm, exhausted but focused in a familiar way that made me smile.

From what I could tell, what I knew about incorporating groundwork in training seemed to be far more than those around me had ever heard of or seen, so it caught the attention of some of the other boarders. Much to my surprise, some asked for my advice with their horses, and with some trepidation, I began teaching a few people. I felt like I could give advice in a way that was more authentic than it had been in the past. It felt less ego-driven and more aligned with the simple desire to help the horses and the people around me. I could see in the riders that *they didn't know what they didn't know*, and having been there myself, I wanted to show them new ways to be more understanding of their horses' behaviors. I was inspired by their eagerness to learn and began to look forward to the regular lessons I taught each week.

In my second summer with Blue, I took him out to some unrated three-phase events, and when those went well, we tried our hand at some rated ones. It had been a long time since I had gone to a horse trials, and I felt like a fish out of water. Rules had changed and jumps looked bigger than I remembered. In Maine, I was closer to venues in New Hampshire and Vermont than the events I had frequented when I was younger, so getting the lay of the land was daunting. Despite these challenges, Blue and I did well that first season together, taking home several top-three finishes. He trusted me, and I felt like we had a genuine connection, which was something I hadn't had with a horse in a long time.

And then our second winter together rolled around. We moved to a new barn with a bigger indoor, and Blue was much fitter than he had ever been. As the weather got colder, he began to have days when he would explode while I was riding, bucking and bolting around the ring. I could feel his tension in the work, but I couldn't predict when an episode was coming. Sometimes it would happen out of nowhere, and sometimes I would expect it the whole ride, and it would never come. I kept thinking I could ride through the tension "to the other side," and that Blue would settle into his "normal" way of going. But by the third unpredictable month, my nerves were raw, and I was leaving the arena in tears after almost every ride. The thing I had brought into my life to be joyful and fun, just for me, had become anxiety-provoking and disappointing. I had two young children to care for, and I did not want to get hurt. I also had a large enough ego story going that I was upset about not being able to fix Blue's issues. I knew I did not have the proper tools in my toolbox, but I didn't even know what those tools might be or where to begin looking for them.

I talked with Steve honestly about the position I found myself in. I was not having fun riding my horse, and I didn't know what to do to improve the situation. It seems strange now, given what we have learned about physical issues' impact on equine behavior, that neither of us jumped on the idea of exploring a physical explanation for Blue's behavior, like ulcers or saddle fitting. I had added magnesium to his diet to help with muscle tension, and it seemed to have some effect, but not enough to make riding him feel safe, and my budget for a deep-dive exploration with a veterinarian was just not there.

Steve, as always, was honest with his opinion. He did not see Blue as particularly athletic or holding much potential beyond Novice level eventing and low-level dressage. He felt my choices were to strip back all the training I had put in thus far and see where the holes in his foundation might be, or to try and find a new home for Blue. I felt daunted by and unsure about the first option, assuming that if I had missed things the first time, I would probably miss them again, and maybe end up right back in the same place. And I wasn't sure if the second option was even possible considering his current behavior, as I could not sell Blue in good conscience without disclosing the issues we were having, and I couldn't buy another horse without selling him for enough money to purchase one.

It was the worst-case scenario: not only was I heartbroken because I truly loved Blue and the journey we had been on together, but I felt trapped by our current situation.

Steve was friends with a family in Massachusetts who bought and sold a lot of horses, and he suggested I contact them about trading Blue for another horse. Steve knew the brothers of the family to have a good eye for quality horses, and in fact, I had once helped a client purchase and bring along a lovely Warmblood gelding who had come through them. With Steve's encouragement, I reached out and gave one of the brothers all the facts about Blue. He listened carefully and was understanding about the situation, noting that, given that Blue's most extreme behavior only seemed to crop up in the winter, the idea of him heading south was the best plan—and he already had a buyer in mind. This was positive news, but did they have a horse that was a fair trade for Blue that would also suit me? We agreed it was worth my looking at a few they had at the time.

When I brought Blue down to Massachusetts, the brothers were quite surprised at his level of training. It was correct in many ways, and he was on his best behavior that day, so all the hours of training Blue and I had logged together showed. He was a nicer horse than they often dealt with or had been expecting, given our conversation the week prior, and they felt confident in making a trade, as Blue was worth more than anything they had on the property. This meant that I had potentially more to lose in any deal we made than they did, but I really didn't have any other viable options that I could see.

I looked at a few horses that were not suitable, and then a chestnut with a runny nose caught my eye. He looked like an Appendix-Quarter Horse—definitely not a full Thoroughbred, which was all right by me, considering what I was trying to move away from. He was a surprisingly good mover, which I hoped meant that he would be more athletically inclined than Blue had been. He was very green, but willing, so after a short ride, I made the trade. I began second-guessing myself the moment I signed the contract. I cried all the way home, wondering if I had just made a terrible mistake, and feeling a tremendous amount of guilt for having simply left Blue at a totally unknown farm with unfamiliar people and routines. That second-guessing continued when my new mount bucked me off the first time I sat on him at his new home. I had named him Unexpected, "Eddie" for short, because of the way his movement had surprised me when I first saw him go. It turned out there were *a lot* of things about him that would be unexpected, from the fact that once he was physically healthy, he was cold-backed and girthy, to the slow discovery that he was more sensitive and anxious than any horse that I had ever worked with.

Even though it had been my decision to make the trade, I mourned the loss of Blue deeply. I worried endlessly about where he would end up, which was something I had never done with the horses I'd helped sell in the past. It was different with Blue because he was meant to be mine for the long haul. He was, in many ways, *my first horse*, and I'd had high hopes for our time together.

I didn't know what to do with the contradicting feelings of believing that trading Blue was the right choice for me, and that I also missed him with all my heart. I sought the support of my 3 Doors Academy mentor, Marcy. She encouraged me to allow myself to feel the sadness I had not been allowing myself to feel because I felt I had no right to, being the one who had chosen to part ways with Blue. With her prompting, I remembered I could use my meditation practice to help process my grief, rather than just trying to move on and shove my sadness down. It was a process—Blue would continue to pop into my mind at random moments, all the time at first, and then less and less often as months passed. When he came to mind at first, it was with tears and a pit of guilt in my stomach, and later it was with just a hint of sadness and regret.

Three years after I'd parted ways with Blue, I found out that he had gone to Florida from the farm in Massachusetts, as intended, and that a hunter trainer there had sold him to a young rider in Pennsylvania. She and her family tracked me down and reached out to me on Facebook to share pictures and stories. They loved Blue dearly. He was clearly pampered and adored and did his job well. He was admired at the shows they attended, and they were so grateful for the good start he'd had with me. They said he still did some silly things when the cold weather hit, but they loved him anyway.

I cried buckets of tears when I got the family's message, the relief of knowing he was safe and loved flooding through me and finally allowing that tight ball of worry I had been holding in my heart to fully release.

It often seems like the universe puts the same messages in front of you until you are ready to open your eyes and truly receive them. The big one for me as I transitioned from working with Blue to Eddie was the ever-familiar "you don't know what you don't know" with a dash of "you need to figure that shit out, for everyone's sake." Though their behaviors were slightly different, both horses had behaviors I didn't have the tools to manage. I, Blue, and Eddie were all doing the best we could with the information we had at the time. It just wasn't enough information to create the positive changes I was looking for in any of us.

As a result of my personal meditation practice, I found that I had more empathy in my life in general, and luckily, empathy breeds patience. When you can truly put yourself in the shoes of others, and see their struggles as if they are your own, you cannot help but be more patient with them as they try to navigate their lives. Though I felt weary at the idea of starting over again with another new horse as I tried to move toward my rekindled lofty eventing goals, I chose to see working with Eddie as a learning opportunity. I put my ambitious thoughts of moving up the levels aside and turned toward gathering more tools for my toolbox. I could clearly see that the skills I had been relying on for so many years just weren't enough to help Eddie, and I could also now see that there were many horses in the world like him, owned by people who had an even smaller skill set than I did. I could potentially help these people, as I grew my own knowledge base and understanding, and that would, in turn, help all their horses. I thought maybe there could be a sort of ripple effect that would eventually help more horses and people than I might ever even know about.

With this little spark of possibility in my heart and mind, I chose to make the move away from social work and back to horses full-time. Through my continued personal meditation practice, and the support of The 3 Doors Academy community and mentors from the program, I felt I had the personal reflection skills necessary to do things differently than I had done them before. I felt a renewed joy in teaching basic things to people who were excited to learn them. I loved watching horses and humans grasp new concepts, and I felt very little desire to "prove myself" in my corner of the horse world. I could see more and more how humans' "stuff" impeded their ability to communicate effectively with their horses, even though improving this communication was their deepest desire, as I clearly recognized my "stuff" had done to me. I still didn't have a clear plan of action or process to bring all the work I had done on myself into my life with horses. I knew there was a path somewhere, but I could not see the steps to it. I just kept trusting that things would evolve as they should if I stayed open and aware and kept tending to my inner journey.

I began to see where my own presence and carefully cultivated ability to stay grounded (and be aware of my groundedness) had a natural impact on the people and horses around me. I experimented with bringing direct meditation experiences into riding lessons—without calling it "meditation." I helped guide riders to focus on the moment-to-moment sensations of their horses' movement and breathing, which allowed them to become more aware of the signals their horses were always sending, in subtle ways. I incorporated more of what I knew about groundwork into all my sessions, because I found that I could read myself and the horses better from the ground than I could from their backs. I could watch their bodies, and more importantly, their eyes, and learned to trust my sense of where the horses were, emotionally and physically. I stopped putting myself in possibly unsafe or compromising situations on horses' backs because I thought I should be able to "ride through it" and would choose to get down and help the horse from the ground instead. I relied on my instincts more and felt confident helping horses that fell at different points on the usual training spectrum. At the same time, I knew there was a ton I still didn't know, especially about how to help horses that fell outside of a certain "norm."

In my early twenties, I had thought I had transitioned from student to teacher, and I had assumed that was a one-way ticket. Maybe I'd thought this because I'd lived in a place without access to regular training for myself, or maybe it was because my working student experience had left a bad taste in my mouth. Whatever the reason, somehow, I'd thought my major "learning phase" was over. It's shocking to acknowledge that now, as my values around continuing education are so strong. I tell all my clients, "Never stop being a student. Never stop seeking knowledge."

Don't let your ego get in the way of becoming better at the things you are passionate about. That is the fastest way to put a big glass ceiling above yourself. You will end up stuck in the same spot, wondering why you keep hitting the same roadblocks. As I learned through personal experience, that is a recipe for bitterness and burnout. When something isn't working, stop banging your head against that ceiling. Don't be afraid to try something different. Take a leap. Do it, knowing for sure that it won't be the last time you seek answers outside your own knowledge base. Do it, knowing that at least it represents some kind of movement, and that's *always* better than stagnation.

18
FINDING PERSPECTIVE

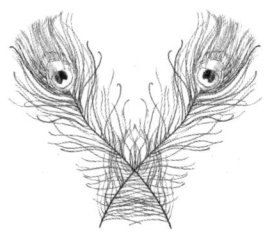

IN 2018, I WENT to the Equine Affaire horse exposition in West Springfield, Massachusetts, with a group of my own clients for the first time. I had attended the year prior and ridden Blue in two clinics with Phillip Dutton at the event, but I hadn't been a professional then, so I saw it as a personal experience rather than a business one. I rode my client Kyra's young horse, Winston, in two dressage clinics in 2018, and several other students came to watch and learn as well. I went into the experience like a sponge, ready to absorb as much information as I could about as many different disciplines and ways of thinking about horses as the event had to offer.

An acquaintance from Maine was a demo rider for a clinician I had never heard of. His name, Tik Maynard, confused me—was his first name pronounced "tick" like the insect or "teak" like the wood? (It's the former.) He taught both jumping and groundwork, which caught my attention because of my own attempts to integrate the two.

The first clinic of his that I made it to was a groundwork session, and I could not take my eyes off what he was doing in the ring. When Tik worked with a horse, it was like the audience didn't exist. He watched each horse so carefully and intently, looking for the slightest suggestion of understanding. He demonstrated a level of patience and consistency that I had never seen, as well as genuine joy when horses figured things out. I was enthralled. I felt instantly that Tik was a person I needed to know and learn from. He was combining a clear understanding of how horses learn with an obvious presence of being that held curiosity and openness at the forefront. His business also focused on teaching horses and riders how to progress up the levels of eventing, as he was doing himself. Until that clinic, I hadn't known there were other people in the world who were doing the thing *I* wanted to be doing: choosing a horse-first process that emphasized groundwork and clear communication as a horse advanced through the eventing world.

I literally chased Tik down after that clinic ended. I followed close on his heels through the thick crowds between vendor booths back to where he was signing copies of his newly released book, *In the Middle Are the Horsemen*. I introduced myself, slightly breathless from my jog, and I asked him if he would please come and do a clinic for my clients in Maine. Deep down, I was really asking for myself, because I knew I needed help to better understand Eddie and the other "more complicated" horses who would likely cross my path at some point. To my surprise, he smiled and said, "Sure, here's my number! Call me and we will get something set up."

I watched every other clinic Tik taught at Equine Affaire that weekend, as I started envisioning his visit to Maine, grinning ear to ear with anticipation of and inspiration from the door that had just opened in my life.

That day reminded me that you never know where the leaps you make will lead. Even if you're scared, if your heart tells you to do it, jump—and see what happens. That's what I had done when

I'd answered Beth Baumert's questions during her seminar, when I'd started chatting with the fellow at my bar who had just bought a horse farm in Virginia, when I'd begged for some way to attend The 3 Doors Academy, and when I'd chased Tik down after his clinic. I can honestly say that if I hadn't done any of those things, none of the opportunities that have presented themselves to me in the horse world would have come to be. When I slow down, zoom out, and look back at all that has unfolded since I transferred to a college in Florida, took on running that first farm, and graduated from The 3 Doors Academy, I can hardly believe it. In those moments, it feels surreal. I know I'm doing the thing I've always done—loving horses and learning about them—but it doesn't even feel like the same person is doing it. It feels like different lifetimes with them.

Zooming out in this way can bring such an immediate sense of gratitude and joy that is hard to come by in the day-to-day trials and tribulations of a life. It's like staring down at your phone for a long time, and then suddenly looking up at a clear blue sky that you forgot existed while in the tiny electronic world in your hand. You get an immediate sense of awe and openness, and the feeling that you are connected to a vastness of being that you had been unaware of just a moment before.

I have a sign in my barn that reads *Gratitude Changes Everything*. I found it at a Dollar Store in Florida a couple of winters ago, as I had begun to move horses there and back to Maine by the seasons. I was feeling lonely and isolated at the time, wrestling with homesickness, but at the same time knowing I would be unhappy working outside in the freezing cold for nine hours a day in Maine. I felt guilty for being sad, considering my choices and circumstances, but didn't know how to snap out of it. Then I saw that sign, sitting amongst other wall decor adorned with similarly cliché phrases, and it immediately reminded me of how very much I had to be grateful for. As soon as I read it, my perspective shifted, and my mood lifted. So I bought it and hung it in my tiny rental apartment, where it would remind me every day of just how lucky I was to be there, doing what I loved in the warmth of the Florida sun.

The sign made its way back to Maine with me and now hangs in a spot that you see immediately upon walking in the front door of my barn. When I am having a stressful day, it continues to serve as a reminder to zoom out and recognize how privileged I am. Not only do I get to do what I love for a living, I am surrounded by people who appreciate my work and share my vision of what the horse-human relationship can look like. I have a network of like-minded horse professionals who I call friends and who I can reach out to with ideas or questions whenever I need to. I have a healthy family that supports me on so many levels, and who I love more than I can adequately sum up in words. I have friends to do horsey and non-horsey things with. I live in a peaceful place, have a warm home, food in my fridge, and clean water to drink. I have more of my needs met on a daily basis than a large portion of the world's population will have in their lifetime.

And then, there are the horses…. Every one of them teaches me something about myself, about people, about relationships, about the world, every single day. How did I get so lucky as to be able to spend my days working with these amazing creatures? What did I do to deserve their grace and patience as I learned my craft over these past thirty-plus years?

I have no earthly idea, but man, I am so very fortunate.

19
FINDING COMMUNITY
───────

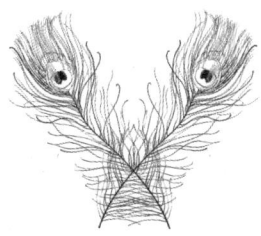

I INVITED TIK TO TEACH in Maine *for myself*. I knew I needed help, and having seen Tik at Equine Affaire, I knew that he offered the kind of guidance I was seeking. And if I am being brutally honest, there was also this little part of me that desperately wanted his approval, in the way that I had so badly wanted to be seen as capable and worthy of being known by those I'd perceived as leaders in the eventing community in my younger years. Thankfully, as the clinic weekend approached, the part of me that simply wanted to learn was louder than that old ego-driven voice.

I wanted everything to be perfect: the footing, the food, the cleanliness of the farm, the schedule, the weather. Shockingly, it all went as well as I could have asked for. I was exhausted the entire time from my preparation efforts, but equally thrilled. I asked Tik endless questions about his methods and kept him at the farm until the very last possible minute before his flight home, working one-on-one with him and Eddie, trying to squeeze every last drop of information out of our time together. I was looking for a step-by-step plan to keep myself moving in the right direction in his absence. Knowing Tik as I do now, I can totally understand why that idea didn't appeal to him, but after that first clinic, I was ready to move to Florida and become a Tik disciple. I felt energized and inspired by his ideas and brainstorming them together on our car rides to and from the farm. And when the clinic was over and Tik had left, I was legitimately depressed. I felt I had so much to work on and now I had the inspiration and more tools to do it well, but I wanted so badly to have that kind of help and interaction regularly... to be a student again! I immediately booked Tik to come back for another clinic in the fall of that same year.

    I determined I would be part of Tik's movement in the horse world, in whatever way I could, because I felt like it was important and happening on a scale I couldn't quite comprehend but could feel. I had the sense things were shifting in the larger horse world and that Tik's work was evidence of that shift. I felt it in myself, and now I was seeing it in others. So when Tik asked if I could help update his website, knowing I had experience in that area through my work for The 3 Doors Academy, I was more than happy to say yes. The work allowed me to stay connected with him and the world he moved in, while utilizing a skill I had to ensure his philosophies and methods became more visible to others. Tik and I met frequently via phone to talk about the website, and he extended an invitation for me to come and visit the farm he and his wife Sinead owned in Citra, Florida that winter.

    I was so excited I could barely stand it!

    The idea for what would become the annual New England Spring Symposium was also born during those phone chats, and we began to plan the inaugural event for May of 2020. I would host both Tik and Sinead for a weekend of learning that was a rarity in my area of the United States. The only USEA-rated event in Maine had stopped running when I was pregnant with Graesyn, and it was clear there was a lack of educational opportunities for the eventing community in my area. Tik and I wanted to make the Symposium something special that people all over New England would put on their yearly calendar, like a mini Equine Affaire. I suggested holding the inaugural event at a premier equine venue in New Gloucester, Maine, called Pineland Farms Equestrian Center, and I went ahead and made the arrangements to rent the space. Pineland had once been the home base for Olympic dressage rider Michael Poulin and was, at the time of our planning, the site of a Morgan history museum and a Morgan breeding program. It offered the space we needed and the quality of host facility we wanted to make the New England Spring Symposium the event we could all picture.

Until the summer of 2019, I had been co-leasing a small farm where another woman and I both ran our training businesses. Between Tik's clinics that year, she let me know that she needed to step away from the space we were sharing. This left me in a tricky position. She and I had been sharing not only the lease but the responsibilities, including caring for the horses, hiring and paying the help, filling in where that help couldn't cover, and generally making sure everything ran as safely and smoothly as possible. The prospect of taking it on completely by myself was incredibly daunting. I didn't know if I wanted that much responsibility on my plate, given I had just returned to being a full-time equine professional again. I was reveling in being a student with more freedom from responsibility. It felt like a slippery slope that I had been avoiding, and taking over the farm on my own would be like diving headfirst down it. But it was either that or try to find someone else to take over the other half of the lease, which would mean sharing the space with someone I didn't necessarily know well or share training philosophies with.

I dove, as I have a habit of doing.

The transition meant I had the unenviable task of figuring out what to do about my former partner's clients, who had boarding spots at the farm. My choices were to allow them to stay at the farm, with my former partner continuing to come there to work with them, or give them the option to either work with me as their trainer or find another farm to move to within a reasonable amount of time. I *hated* that part of the ordeal. I *hated* being the perceived bad guy—being seen as mean or unfair. I wanted everyone to be happy and everyone to like me. At the same time, I needed my business to be sustainable, which was impossible if some of the stalls at the small farm were earning someone else a living. The math just didn't work.

I opted to give everyone the choice to work with me or move on to another farm. Some chose to stay, some chose to go. It was uncomfortable on many levels, but as soon as I had the farm to myself, I was actually glad that things had worked out as they had. I liked having the decision-making power over what happened in the barn and being the sole communicator with the facility owner. I liked the space being filled with *my* clients and their horses, and they all seemed to like it too. The transition meant I could start to think about the kind of clients I really wanted to have and curate the learning environment I could envision as I began to integrate the new training tools I was learning.

When Tik came back to teach in the fall of 2019, we went out to grab a bite to eat and a drink while we rehashed the weekend's activities. I can't remember the question Tik asked that prompted my response to tell him the story of my mom's well-meaning comment, "There will always be someone better than you," but I will never forget his response. Without skipping a beat, he said, "Ah, now it makes sense."

I was confused and asked what he meant.

"You don't know how good you are, do you?" he asked.

I was immediately embarrassed, and said something like, "I don't know what you mean..." Tik rescued me from my discomfort, explaining that he considered me a better trainer than a large majority of professionals he knew because I was not only a very good rider, but I had a keen eye for training with good timing and feel, and I was a clear teacher whose clients made obvious progress. He told me that many professionals he knew were good at one or two of those things, but not all of them.

"I know a lot of great riders and competitors, but they don't necessarily understand training a horse, or they can train but they can't teach. You can do all three really well," he said.

I was beyond flattered, and honestly, in disbelief. It took a long while for what Tik told me to sink in, and even today, I have trouble believing it sometimes. I assume there are other people out there doing what I do *better*, which somehow takes away from how well I am doing it. But I also trust Tik and his opinions. During that time, when I had moments of self-doubt, my dinner conversation with him would pop into my mind and help me reconnect with the self-confidence I needed to make the next decision I was faced with for the horses I was working with.

I rode Eddie in Sinead's clinic at Equine Affaire in November of 2019, shortly after Tik's second visit to my farm. Once I had met and ridden with her, I wanted "in" with their team even more, so when Tik suggested I take him up on his offer to visit their farm, Copperline, and come down to Florida for a clinic they were hosting in January of 2020, I was determined to make it happen. It was a whirlwind trip down to Citra and back for a weekend, but it was worth it. I met a liberty trainer named Dan James, an Australian I was thrilled for the opportunity to learn from, and Tik let me use one of his horses in the sessions. I felt like I was all thumbs and two left feet, but it was the first time I began to really feel my way around the concept of balancing *drive* and *draw* with a horse, the two opposing forces in great liberty work. It felt like magic, and I knew it was another training rabbit hole I wanted to dive into.

Tik also introduced me to a man named Nick Rivera who was developing an online learning platform called The Horseman's University. It was a place where Nick envisioned offering complete, structured courses on a vast array of horsemanship topics in groundwork and riding from top horsepeople in order to support those with limited access to quality equestrian education near them. Nick was, and still is, one of the most unassuming, humble, and kind individuals I have met in the horse world. He was also an excellent horseman, a literal jack of all trades, and a consummate learner, and the idea of his educational platform amazed me. At that time, we had no idea that COVID-19 would shut down the world a few months later and that online learning would become such a huge part of the horse industry. Nick was ahead of his time, in a market that was about to be flooded.

Later that winter, my ride-or-die student, cheerleader, and right-hand organizer of all things, Katie, who had first started working with me at Upper Pond, embarked on an epic road trip with me and my two children, then eight and four, to visit Tik and Sinead over my kids' February school vacation. It was an adventure, to say the least! Twenty-four hours is a long time to contain two children in one minivan. Trying to play and learn with ponies while also keeping the two of them entertained was another balancing act. Thankfully, Tik and Sinead had their own young child at that time, so they understood the delicate dance we were doing and were patient with the energy we brought to their home and farm that week.

While there, I had the opportunity to ride one of Tik's personal competition horses, Galileo, a giant black Warmblood with gaits to die for. At one point, Tik asked me to watch *him* ride the horse and offer him help on the flat. When I had ridden the gelding, I'd found he had a distinct drift through his left shoulder when tracking right. I made that observation to Tik, and he said he didn't feel it, so I was hesitant to offer other ideas, unsure of myself once again.

The next day, Tik took Galileo to a show jumping lesson with David O'Connor, and David ended up sitting on the horse. Within five minutes David shouted over to Tik, "How do you ride this thing with him falling out through his left shoulder all the time?"

My self-satisfaction at that moment was probably palpable in the next county! My feel of the horse had been backed up by one of the best eventing riders and general horsemen of all time. I also enjoyed telling Sinead the story almost as much as the actual moment it had happened, as I was learning that bursting Tik's own self-satisfaction bubble was a favorite household pastime.

The biggest lesson, though, was that the experience reminded me to trust what *I feel* with a horse, even when someone else doesn't feel the same thing.

That trip with Katie also served as an opportunity to make detailed plans for the upcoming inaugural New England Spring Symposium, slated to take place just three months later. One evening, as Tik, Sinead, Katie and I were brainstorming ideas, a conversation started about the different "kinds" of horses in the world. It evolved because I was talking about Eddie and his potential as an event horse. Both Tik and Sinead had helped me with him at that point and knew my horse well.

Sinead said something then that put things in perspective for me: "You can't compare a horse like Eddie to a horse like Galileo…it's like comparing apples to oranges."

I had never thought of horses in that way before. I had not had the opportunity in my life to ride many horses like Galileo. I just assumed that with the "right" work, apples became oranges, and that if they didn't, it was because the apple's trainer lacked the necessary skills. This was also a large component of my self-doubt—I had never been able to turn an apple into an orange, though I thought I should be able to.

Accepting that apples and oranges are two completely different species of fruit and one cannot magically be made into the other, no matter the skill level of the scientist attempting the feat, was a light bulb moment that left me both relieved and confused. Now I had an apple on my hands (I decided Eddie was a Pink Lady, not a Red Delicious, so a fancier apple, but still an apple). What I really wanted for my own personal eventing goals was an orange. Not the fanciest orange out there, but at least some sort of citrus. It would probably have to be a small orange with some bumps and bruises, if I was going to figure out how to afford it. I planted that idea in Tik's mind and asked him to keep his eye out for an orange for me.

That journey home from Florida will not soon be forgotten. Though my son was quite young at the time, even *he* remembers the details of how we stopped for dinner, and the driver's side sliding door literally fell off the van in my hands. My children ran up and down a sidewalk in downtown Richmond, Virginia, burning the pent-up energy of the last nine hours in a vehicle while we waited for hours for AAA. When the technician finally arrived, he was not sure how to get the van door back on, so I took his tools, gave him directions, and somehow managed to wrestle it back into place. We put duct tape over the handle so that none of us would accidentally open it again, for fear it would come off, and got back on the highway to find a place to stay for the night. Within about ten miles, the van began to shudder uncontrollably and threatened to stall. We pulled off the highway, and I called Nick, who advised me to get to a Walmart and buy a car code reader so we could try to determine what was going on. I Googled the codes the reader spit out on my phone, and we learned that the problem was either basically nothing...or something that could potentially kill my engine if I continued to drive the minivan.

Katie and I found a nearby hotel, got the kids to bed, and frantically searched for a one-way rental vehicle big enough to fit all of us and our stuff, and then for a way to get the minivan home without it being driven. Katie was a full-time schoolteacher, as well as my right hand, and had to be back for work in thirty-six hours, so the pressure was high. Somehow, we found a rental and left my van in what we thought would be a safe place, plans for its return to Maine still not fully formed (it followed on a flatbed a week later).

Despite the disastrous ending, I felt the trip was completely worth it...though I have never driven my kids to Florida again.

20
FINDING AN ORANGE

IT WAS AROUND THIS TIME that my wonderful saddle fitter, Joan Riedel of JGR Saddlefit, connected me with the Prestige Italia Ambassador Program. She knew that Tik and Sinead were working with Prestige at the time, and thought that I would be a good fit for the saddlemaker's US-based program. I filled out the application, and with a good word from Joan, I am sure, I was approved. I had my first "sponsor"—something that helped professionals cover the costs of maintaining and performing at high levels while also elevating their profiles—and I was beyond excited! It felt like a dream, and I could not believe I was finally in a position where sponsorship could be a reality. This was also when I began to get another taste of what I now know as "impostor's syndrome": old familiar messages ran through my mind, mixed in with some new one-liners—*Who do you think you are? Why do you deserve this? No way you are good enough.*

The confusing mix of feelings I was experiencing was doubled when a lovely woman named Helena Harris, host of the *Stall and Stable* podcast, asked me to come on her show as a guest. She had audited both the clinics I had hosted with Tik, and we'd had the opportunity to connect at those times. She'd watched me work with horses and students at the clinics, and Tik had suggested to her that I would be a good guest for her show.

Despite my unease related to my new status in the industry, I didn't feel nervous at all during my time recording a conversation with Helena. I loved every second of the interview. Her show was one of the first opportunities I had ever had to tell my story. I was surprised that anyone would want to hear it, frankly, but from what I gathered from the people around me after the podcast went live, my story sounded relatable and genuine, which made it, and me, appealing.

I had learned through repeated experiences that willingness and openness to learning new things would get me farther than a chip on my shoulder and something to prove. When I felt a hint of that familiar desperation to be noticed by Tik and Sinead and the other people in their social circle, I had the tools from my years with The 3 Doors Academy and my personal practice to recognize it for what it was and recalibrate my thoughts toward *learning* rather than being noticed. This brought a level of joy back into the opportunities in front of me. Sure, the hope to be seen and admired was there, quietly under the surface, but the desire to truly understand horses and to help them understand people more clearly and easily was louder than that hope.

Lo and behold, following a genuine path driven by a desire to improve the lives of other beings naturally resulted in real connections with the kind of people I wanted to be associated with, rather than surface-level interactions with names I thought meant something. The kind of people I wanted to be associated with didn't bat an eye at my fumbling and mistakes. They answered my questions with careful thought and genuinely enjoyed horse-nerd discourse. They appreciated my willingness to make mistakes in the name of learning and self-improvement, and they fostered that growth simply by the nature of their own innate desire to learn and improve themselves.

I often encourage students to examine their long-held beliefs about themselves, their equine partners, and horses in general. I gently remind them that those beliefs may not be true, or they may only be partially true, as I have discovered on my own path. Long-standing habits and patterns can seem like the truth simply because you are so familiar with them, but that doesn't make them the *only* truth.

Around this time, a conundrum that I had first discovered in my youth was again confirmed through experience—that is, sometimes two seemingly opposite ideas can both be true at the same time. For example, I began to see that a horse could learn new concepts really well through clear pressure-and-release training...and also through positive-reinforcement training. There were people who used one or the other of those methods exclusively and who believed that the other camp was wrong for various reasons, or that mixing the two was a big no-no. I thought the space in between was more interesting: less black and white, more gray; more curiosity; more exploration and discovery; more flow and feel and learning; more true to the nature of "being," at least as I had experienced it so far.

Another example of this dynamic could be seen when I looked in the mirror: I was a person who was very good at what I did with horses but also a person who made mistakes and had no idea what to do sometimes. As a self-proclaimed perfectionist who some might label as "Type A," this was a tough characteristic for me to acknowledge then, and sometimes still now. But what if I simply accepted that dualism? Wouldn't that be a much nicer way to live with myself? To have a deep-seated belief in my own abilities and in my work, but to also know that it's okay if I don't know everything, all the time?

Revolutionary. Freeing. It turns out that self-limiting is a useless habit, and so is self-deprecation. I have seen and felt the evidence over and over again in my own life and in the lives of those around me. Whenever I can remember to hold the seemingly opposite aspects of my being—both the excellence and the imperfection—in the same open space of understanding and awareness, I am automatically more joyful and free to move through my life with grace for myself and others, equine and human alike.

These realizations were building as I worked with my team to prepare everything for the 2020 New England Spring Symposium. The venue was rented, the necessary insurance purchased, the riders selected, the clinicians' plane tickets were waiting in their email inboxes, and the eventing community of New England was primed to have Tik and Sinead teaching together in our little neck of the woods. When the COVID lockdown hit in March of 2020, we held out hope that by May, things would be back to normal. We sent emails and created social media posts telling people things were still "on," until we were faced with the depressing fact that cancellation was the only option. It was devastatingly disappointing, as were so many things during that time of everyone's lives. Momentous gatherings of all kinds were canceled. The childhood events my kids didn't get to experience broke my heart in two. My riding clients faced possible layoffs and loss of income, and all of a sudden my husband and I had to manage him working from home along with two young children who we were trying to help figure out remote learning.

I wasn't the only one who thought COVID was the perfect time to get a puppy.

I had decided I wanted another Boxer in my life, having had one for a decade. We'd lost Taylor to lymphoma a few years prior. One of my clients sent me a Facebook ad for unregistered Boxer puppies in Boston. I called the number and asked if they would please hold one for me; then Katie, always ready for an adventure, and I jumped in the car and arrived in Boston two hours later to pick up the only puppy left. The eight-week-old female hadn't been picked by anyone else because she was shy and hung back, while her siblings had been more extroverted. I loved that about her and knew I would have picked her even if her brothers and sisters had been there to climb on me first. She was perfect, and I named her Willow after seeing a street with that name right near where we picked her up. She slept in my arms all the way home.

Willow became my instant sidekick, accompanying me to the farm every day from then on, gaining fans wherever we went together. She was a bright light in a dark time, like so many puppies were for people that year.

Then there was a horse. My first orange.

Tik called me one day and said, "I think I found a horse for you." The details were vague: a gray gelding, on the smaller side, Warmblood of some sort, supposedly five years old, a dressage flunky who had just started dabbling in eventing with the trainer who owned the farm where Tik and Sinead then rented a house. Tik sent me videos and described him as a "Ferrari with a touchy gas pedal." Given the sensitivity of the horses Tik had helped me with, he thought I could manage the little gray gelding, and that his athleticism was worth the try.

Over the course of the next week, I was told that Little Einstein was actually six—and then, wait, actually *seven*. This gave me a little leverage to at least haggle with the owner over the asking price, knowing precisely how much cash I had been squirreling away in my closet for the prior two years, and guessing how much a pre-purchase exam and shipping would cost me.

I scheduled the pre-purchase exam, and when he passed, without ever having sat on him or met him in person (because people weren't getting on airplanes then), I bought him and had him shipped to Maine. Terrifyingly, I had bought him based on the advice of my friend and a veterinarian I had only ever talked to on the phone—and it was the largest lump sum of cash I had ever paid for anything in my life.

The gray was smaller than I expected when he arrived, but he was the fanciest horse I had ever owned or imagined owning. He was sound and pretty sane and a fantastic mover with a scopey jump, and he was all mine! I called him "Albert," a play on his show name, Little Einstein, and I couldn't believe my good fortune. I cried tears of joy hacking him around the farm with relaxed ease, reveling in his willingness, try, and athleticism.

At the exact same time, recognizing that I did not need, nor could I afford, two horses, I was crying tears of guilt and sadness as I advertised and subsequently sold Eddie. Thankfully he went to a wonderful home, where his new adult amateur owner thought he was the most perfect horse she could ever have purchased. It was (and continues to be) an ideal home for Eddie with the best owner either of us could have asked for, but I found it was still gut-wrenching to see him go. The new way I was working with horses forged a kind of emotional connection with them that was much harder to sever than the "working relationship" I'd had with so many in the past. You couldn't have paid me to go back to the way I had done things before, but it made it *much* harder to have horses come in and out of my life.

During the pandemic, I was fortunate to be in a line of work that I could continue, mostly because the farm lent itself easily to social distancing. There was a period of time when I organized clients coming to the farm in shifts, one at a time, so that there was little-to-no contact between people. I was doing more training rides than teaching lessons, and there was a sense of quiet on the premises that was sometimes a welcome respite from the craziness of the larger world. I had a lot of clients in health care, and the stories they brought to the farm were like something out of a dystopian novel. They couldn't believe what they were seeing at the hospitals, and their obvious fear and stress was disconcerting. My children were doing their best with online learning, but they were too young to be engaged with a teacher via a small screen for long periods of time, and the lack of social connections with peers was taking its toll on them. Nick was doing his best to keep up with working from home, but when the kids were done with schoolwork each day, they looked to him for attention and boredom relief. Thank goodness my mother and stepfather lived nearby and were willing and able to support us and our children that year...we all would have lost our minds without them.

I brought Tik up to my farm twice for small, private clinics during 2020, and in between his visits, he continued to be a sounding board for me as I forged my new relationship with Albert. I was grateful I also had the opportunity to return the favor and be a support to Tik, as a person from whom he could seek advice. Tik called me one afternoon out of the blue, upset about the comments people were making online after he did a demo for the Retired Racehorse Project at a big event in Florida. He and two other trainers had been invited to talk about and demonstrate how they would start a Thoroughbred right off the track, looking to move the horse into the eventing world. The trainers had no say in the horses they got to work with—it was a random draw—and the horse Tik had been assigned was not shy about invading his personal space. The Thoroughbred had seemed to have a high tolerance for pressure and was not all that interested in giving Tik any of his focus or attention. Tik had a rope halter, fourteen-foot rope, and flag to work with, and he'd had to "get pretty big" with the flag several times to keep the horse he was handling at a safe distance from him.

The comments viewers had posted in response to the online video shared by the Retired Racehorse Project after the event chided Tik for his use of the flag around the horse's face and had sent Tik into a hole of self-doubt. Firstly, the fact that Tik was vulnerable to that kind of uncertainty surprised me, and at the same time, I could clearly relate to it. Secondly, the fact that he'd called me for advice at that moment felt important, so I took the task very seriously. I listened as Tik explained his fear and frustration over the situation, and I reminded him that there were always going to be "haters" out there. I suggested that all he could do was learn from the situation and encouraged him to ignore the "trolls" of the internet world and focus on building skills that would serve him better if he were ever in a similar position again.

A few months later, I read an article Tik had written for *The Chronicle of the Horse* where he referenced our conversation, and

I was taken aback. How could this person I admired and respected be looking back at *me* with admiration and respect? The only answer I had was what I had stumbled upon in earnest when I first saw Tik at Equine Affaire—he and I were in genuine alignment with a shared larger vision and greater purpose in the horse world. And if there were two of us out there, I allowed myself to imagine there must be more.

21
FINDING HOME

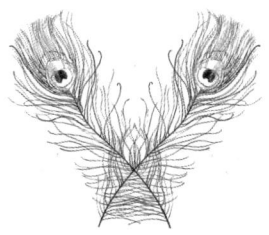

IN THE SUMMER OF 2020, the owner of the farm I was leasing, Amanda, posed a question to me: "Why are you spending all this money renting my farm, when you could be putting that money into something you own?"

At first, I thought, *There's literally no way we could afford to do that. I just spent my 'closet money' on a new horse and we have no savings for a down payment.* Amanda was a realtor and encouraged me to connect with a lending agent she often worked with, and through a conversation with him, and then subsequent conversations with other lending agents and banks, along with some serious discussions with Nick about the viability of such a plan, we actually began looking at farm properties for sale in Maine. After looking at things from every angle, the options I had were to stay small, where I was, with the space and amenity limitations of the farm I was leasing, or find another place to lease that would allow my business to grow, *or* find our own farm to both live and work on, which would allow my business to truly expand. The possibility of growth felt real at that time, and the idea of owning our own space had far more appeal to both of us than staying in the same situation for the foreseeable future.

After visiting two properties in southern Maine that didn't particularly appeal to us, we put in an offer for a third farm close to where my parents lived. Much to our disappointment, our offer was rejected, and the farm was sold to someone else. So we were back to the drawing board. One afternoon, Nick sent me an ad for a farm north of where we were living at the time, and I immediately dismissed it. It was literally the worst real estate ad I had ever seen—the photos were blurry and had random people and a lot of junk in them. But Nick persisted with the idea that we take a look, because the price was right.

When I looked at the listing a little more closely, I realized that I had been to that farm years prior, with some clients who'd been in the market. It had a unique, three-story round barn that I had been enthralled by. Nick and I made a plan to go look in person.

It was far from perfect. The farm had no indoor or outdoor riding arena, barely any fencing, and the house on the property was clearly in disrepair. *But the barn*…the barn was amazing and unusual, and I could picture myself in it. There was also a half-mile track on the property, and it was only five minutes from Interstate 95, which I knew would be useful for clients and for Nick's commute to work. It had the bones of a place that we could make into something amazing.

Little did I know when we started the process of trying to purchase the property that I would basically have to earn associate's degrees in accounting, commercial lending, and business planning. Let me just say, math is *not* my strong suit, and I had to do *a lot* of math to make the whole thing work. I had to figure out how to navigate the Small Business Administration, along with its various lending institutes and red tape, as well as local banks and their requirements for commercial lending. We needed the funds to not only purchase the property, but to also build indoor and outdoor arenas and install fencing, and I had to prove to multiple lenders that the business I would conduct there was not only viable but scaleable with the improvements we intended to make with the loans we were asking for. The whole thing got very complicated, really quickly, and became a fourth job—beyond the farm, my continuing part-time work for The 3 Doors Academy, and raising two children. I stayed up until the wee hours of the morning trying to figure out things like business plans, balance sheets, and financial projections with the help of Google, through exhausted tears of frustration. I spent every spare minute between clients during the day calling for excavation and building quotes, and hitting dead ends, time after time. But I persisted.

Nick and I told no one about the potential farm purchase—not even our families. Some of my long-time clients were aware of the possibility, but not many. With Amanda's help, we quietly put our house on the market, and thankfully, it was during the pandemic when literally everyone and their brother was trying to find a house to buy in the country. Within days, our little house was worth double what we'd paid for it, and we were getting offers well over what we were asking.

A perfectly aligned series of events had to take place for the rundown farm with the incredible barn in Wales, Maine, to become ours—and somehow, they did. We got an offer on our house, the offer we made on the farm was accepted, we were approved for loans through the SBA and a local Maine bank, we had people lined up to build the indoor and outdoor arenas, and the woman selling the farm was approved for her own loan to purchase a different property.

Amanda, who acted as our realtor, could not believe that everything fell into place. It was literally a miracle, by all accounts, and the process had Nick and me on the edge of nervous breakdowns. Looking back, I still cannot believe it all came together, even knowing the amount of effort I had put into making it happen.

In late August of 2020, we signed the paperwork. *The farm was ours.*

We decided to call the property Unexpected Farm. This was in part after my horse Eddie, whose show name had been Unexpected, and who seemed to have started me down the road that had led to this major life upheaval. He had been the impetus for my chasing Tik down four years prior at Equine Affaire, which had been when the real changes in my professional life had started. The other reason we called it Unexpected Farm was because we'd had absolutely *no* intention of buying a farm just a few months prior. The whole thing was genuinely shocking in its unfolding.

On the first of September, we moved to our new farm—and I cried every day for the three months following. I started most days regretting the decision we had made, missing my simple, organized life. The house was an absolute mess, even more so than we'd believed. The four of us lived in our camper for almost a month, and when we finally moved into the house, it was really just into the bedrooms, as the kitchen wouldn't be renovated for several more months. Much to our dismay, we found we needed to rebuild the entire floor structure under one end of the house because the floor joists literally crumbled in Nick's hands when he touched them. We found more rot, broken pipes, and cut corners every time we started a new project—in the house or barn—and this was all happening at the same time our children were trying to acclimate to an entirely new school district while doing partial online and partial in-school learning. Nick was working half from home and half in his company office, and I was continuing to run my business out of the farm I still leased, thirty-five minutes from Unexpected. I drove to work with horses and clients after getting my kids to school in the mornings, came home eight or nine hours later to feed them and get them to bed, then worked online for The 3 Doors Academy while trying not to fall asleep at my laptop. I usually then rallied to do several hours of work on the house until one or two in the morning, finally falling asleep before my head even hit the pillow, and then started the whole thing over again the next day.

On the weekends, Nick and I worked from sunup until after dark, trying to get paddocks built and the barn sorted out so that horses could move in by the first of March, because that's when finances demanded that I no longer pay both a lease and a new mortgage. We were ghosted by multiple contractors in the process of trying to get the indoor built during a Maine winter, and we had to complete the work of others who claimed their job was done when it clearly was not. Neither of us slept much for the better part of eight months, and I lost fifteen pounds, which left me weighing what I had in high school, almost twenty years prior. It was not healthy, and I was often not happy. But I had a vision and the drive to bring it to life. The phrase from the movie *Field of Dreams*, "If you build it, they will come," was on repeat in my mind, and despite the extreme uphill climb in the direction of my vision, I felt sure I was doing what I was meant to be.

Everyone we knew cheered us on and helped whenever they could. My parents, Nick's family, and our friends volunteered countless hours helping us with hard labor tasks like putting in fence posts and building kick walls in the indoor. Tik came and taught a clinic at the leased farm in October of 2020, but stayed with us at Unexpected. He could see the vision I had, and his words of encouragement gave me stamina to keep pushing on. We literally could not have brought things together in the timeframe we did without all the people in our corner.

On March first of 2021, we moved horses from the farm I had been leasing to Unexpected Farm, in a late winter snowstorm.

Nick Rivera came to film a course for The Horseman's University with me in April, a flattering idea that he and Tik had presented me with a few months prior. We had the bones of the course laid out ahead of his visit, and made the final plans together on the third floor of the barn, overlooking the property and the lake across the road. We enlisted my clients to be part of the filming, and wove together concepts of meditation and horsemanship into a course we hoped would be a fresh perspective on problem-solving with horses by focusing on the handler's ability to be aware and present first, and second, by practicing specific techniques for developing better feel and timing. In the few days he was with us, Nick also helped us level our indoor arena footing and unstick our very stuck brand-new tractor by "borrowing" our contractor's excavator and pulling it out with the bucket arm, much to my and my husband's relief! His physical help and effusive support for my work was just what I needed in those early days.

Tik, Sinead, Katie, and I had moved the postponed inaugural New England Spring Symposium to May of 2021 at Unexpected Farm, so we had a serious deadline to meet soon after moving the horses in, considering the hundred-plus people we were expecting at the event. My stress level was through the roof as I dealt with an often-unreliable excavator who was meant to be finishing the outdoor arena necessary to have both Tik and Sinead teaching at the same time during the Symposium. It was completed only three days prior to the event start date, along with painting the road-facing sides of the property buildings, mowing long-overgrown grassy areas all over the farm, weeding and mulching gardens at the front of the property, and readying the barn for tours of its three unique levels.

The whole event weekend was stressful, to say the least, but also a euphoric culmination of all our efforts. Looking around at the farm during the Symposium, watching my boarders and students proudly helping the visitors we were hosting, I had the ongoing sensation of living a dream. How could this all be *ours*? How could this be *my life*? It was another example of two opposite truths existing in the same place at the same time: I was exhausted and was doing the hardest things I had ever done in my life, but I was also the happiest and felt the most alive and satisfied that I ever had. I was living in constant amazement at what I was capable of and what the universe had to offer.

Soon after the Symposium, Tik introduced me to Caroline Culbertson, an equestrian who had worked with Tik to produce content for a new online equestrian education platform called Noelle Floyd Masterclass. Caroline had recently moved to Maine and was looking for help with a mare she had been struggling to connect with for a long time. Caroline sent her horse, Ellie, to me for training, and I quickly understood what she had been experiencing. Ellie was an extremely sensitive horse with a propensity to go through the motions without really knowing what her handler was asking. She was quick to become tense and anxious, and was very gate- and herd-bound in the arena. I started working with Ellie on the ground in ways that were unfamiliar to Caroline, and that piqued her interest. I made some significant progress with Ellie and helped Caroline understand the mare's actions in ways she had never before.

Having witnessed the positive results of my work with her mare, Caroline was kind enough to bring my name to her employer, Noelle Floyd, and suggested the team film several Masterclasses with me. Caroline also jumped on board as one of my biggest supporters, and we made an arrangement to trade part of Ellie's training for Caroline's help with my website, social media, and advertising. Caroline became my agent, and her vast experience and professionalism helped my business tremendously. She got my name out to potential sponsors and talked me up to other people she knew from her time in the industry. She hosted me on her award-winning podcast, *Equestrian Voices*, and soon Katie and I began to joke that I was becoming "moderately famous in the general New England area."

As you have seen throughout these pages, my life has been a continual lesson in being open to possibility. I can't overstate the power of this for yourself and your horses. Put your dreams and desires out to the universe. It's wild what will present itself that you may not even be able to imagine. If I had dismissed Amanda's suggestion of buying a farm rather than being open to the idea, no matter how far-fetched or unrealistic it seemed at the moment, none of what has transpired in my life with horses since then would have been possible. Every time I find myself getting attached to an idea or a plan, or disappointed when one doesn't work out in the way I expected, I try to remember to take a breath and open outward, rather than shut down and turn inward. I remember all the times that one small thing has led to another and another in ways I never could have predicted or even hoped for. More times than not, the outcome ended up being better than the one I was hoping for, or it has led to some lesson I didn't even know I needed to learn. That doesn't mean I don't work for what I envision or believe in, clearly. It just means there's a balance.

I've explained that I find riding, and life in general, are both made up of a constant balancing act between the opposite sides of hundreds of different coins. Every time I teach a lesson and I talk about the need for the balance of opposing concepts like drive and draw or collection and extension, I am reminded of the same needs in me. The balance of hustle and flow, of determination and flexibility. Because when I attend to those balances, that's when I find the most ease of movement in my life, as we find ease of movement in our horses when they are in balance within themselves and with us. This is also where unexpected possibilities seem to present themselves.

Perfect balance is very hard to strike—in life and on horses. Sometimes you will be way out of whack, and if you know it's temporary, it's okay...you just can't stay that way forever, or you'll burn out and possibly harm the people around you. Sometimes I get pretty far out of balance, and it takes someone else pointing out my struggle to wake me up and tip me upright again. I try to heed their concerns and recalibrate, even when it's difficult to course-correct, because momentum in a given direction is very powerful. Getting out of balance happens and will continue to happen to all of us. It is a normal part of our human existence, and there's no use in berating ourselves when we are tipping. What's important is that we look around once in a while, notice what is out of balance, and make the conscious effort to change.

22
FINDING A RHYTHM

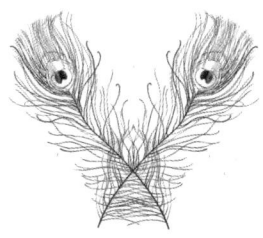

THE FIRST YEAR I had Unexpected Farm in operation, I lined up dressage Olympian Laura Graves to come give a clinic in August. I had the good fortune to have a client who had sent a horse to her for training, and that client generously sent me to Laura for some lessons on her horse before he came back to Maine. I made the clinic suggestion to Laura when I was with her in Florida, and being a fellow New Englander (she grew up in Vermont), she was open to the idea of coming back up to that area of the country.

When word got out that Laura was teaching at my farm, representatives from the one-time print magazine and now-online media outlet *Dressage Today* reached out to me about covering the event and asked if I would appear on their podcast in the leadup to the clinic. Caroline pitched them the idea of filming some of my work, if they were already going to be at my farm, and they went for it—both *Dressage Today* and its sibling print magazine and online outlet *Practical Horseman* had platforms looking for groundwork content, and *Practical Horseman* wanted some simple jumping lessons for its online library. A tentative plan was also made to reconnect with the *Practical Horseman* team in Ocala that winter for further filming.

Ultimately, the two clinics held in our first year at Unexpected Farm brought a great deal of attention to the space, my work with horses, and my mission to bring high-quality education to an area of the United States that often lacks access to quality trainers. It was an opportunity for people in the Northeast, and beyond, to be introduced to my training philosophies and processes. Coupled with podcast interviews and filming online content for three different educational platforms, I was beginning to build a brand and a reputation based on work I truly believed in and was driven to continue for sustainable and heartfelt reasons.

I was also having great success competing Albert in his first season of eventing at the Beginner Novice level, winning almost every event we entered. That November, I rode him with three amazing clinicians at Equine Affaire in Massachusetts: the legendary Olympian and eventing coach Jimmy Wofford, liberty trainer (and my new friend) Dan James, and Karen Rohlf, founder of Dressage Naturally. It was an amazingly diverse group of people to learn from, and Albert was an absolute star in all three arenas. I made a plan to move up to Novice level that winter—in Florida.

Unexpected Farm was feeling settled enough toward the end of 2021 that I felt I could take the step I had been wanting to for years and do a winter competition season in Florida—a common means for northern-based equestrians to keep their horses progressing when the weather at their home base became a challenge. I took Albert and two clients and their horses to Ocala in January, planning to stay until the end of March 2022. I had found a place to board the horses near the HITS Ocala showgrounds and a small apartment to rent in Citra, near Tik and Sinead's farm. The barn where the horses were kept was the full-time location for another professional who evented at the upper levels. She and her clients were horse showing almost every weekend beginning in mid-January, and I felt a twinge of that old familiar anxiety of wanting to fit in but identifying as "an outsider" in the high-performance world. Despite this, I stuck to my values and worked the horses I'd brought on the ground in rope halters, as much if not more than I rode them, garnering some sideways glances from the farm regulars.

I was able to go to Tik and Sinead for regular lessons, and as a testament to our work together, Albert and I won our first Novice competition of that season at Rocking Horse, the location of my horse show nightmare when I had been a working student for Darren Chiacchia. I filmed the Masterclasses for Noelle Floyd, which I felt well-prepared for, and which by all accounts went splendidly. During the day, things were going very well, though I was quite lonely in my little apartment every night. I distracted myself with unhealthy habits like Netflix bingeing, ice cream, and wine at the end of the day, and then balanced things out with meditation each morning.

On one particular early-morning drive to the farm, as I watched the sun come up over a field dotted with majestic live oak trees draped with Spanish moss, and sang along with a mantra melody by my 3 Doors Academy mentor Marcy, tears spontaneously sprang to my eyes as a wave of gratitude for everything in my life swept over and engulfed me. That feeling was as beautiful as the sunrise I was watching, and profound in its power to lift my spirits, reminding me again of the things most important to me. This was an inner strength I would need as life began balancing all the good with new challenges, as it so often does.

One of the girls who traveled to Ocala with me that winter, Sophia, was a long-term client who was on a gap year after graduating high school. The other was still in high school and not a regular client, but rather a young rider who had participated in the New England Spring Symposium and whose mother had expressed interest in sending her to Florida for the winter season. I'd offered her a spot to travel with me, given her positive experience with Tik and Sinead, and hoped she would embrace my program and the help I could provide. Unfortunately, this young lady balked at my suggestions, talked back during lessons, and watched the other professional and her students at the farm with obvious longing.

About six weeks into our time in Ocala, the young rider and her mother let me know that she wanted to start riding with the other trainer at our barn. It was a huge slap in the face and a devastating blow to my ego. I knew how much I had to offer this student and her horses, and I was beyond frustrated that she was overlooking the potential in my program for the "shiny thing" nearby. It was a real test of my confidence and belief in my processes to remain at the farm with this young lady working with the other trainer for the rest of the season. I had to dig deep in my personal practice in order to allow space for the voices of doubt and hurt in my mind to be acknowledged, but not to take me over. Sometimes I was successful, and other times I got sucked into the familiar stories of "not good enough." It was a learning experience I was not planning to have when I had headed south, but it did eventually leave me with a greater clarity about what was important to me and what was not. It confirmed in me that my process was more important than how I was perceived or the outward immediacy of its results.

As the season progressed, Albert seemed to be growing more anxious and even uncomfortable in his work. I wondered if it was because we had moved up a level and the questions I was asking were getting a bit more complicated. He started having confidence issues in show jumping schools both at our home farm and away at lessons, which culminated in him injuring himself on the jump fill under an oxer at a clinic with British Olympian William Fox Pitt. Albert was out of commission for several weeks while the skin healed under the stitches he'd received. I took the opportunity to have him scoped for ulcers, as his behavior seemed different than I had experienced with him before.

The scope confirmed what I had suspected—grade two ulcers—and Albert went on an intensive treatment regimen for twenty-eight days. But even after his pastern wound healed and his ulcer treatment neared its end, Albert's confidence was still low. It was a struggle to get him around a Novice course. I could tell he was only jumping because I told him he had to and that he was not feeling the ease and enjoyment I had felt in him the prior summer. I knew this was antithetical to the way I wanted to be working with horses. I did not want to make the same mistakes I had made with Lucy.

I decided I had to go home and realign myself, for both our sakes, even if it meant giving up a portion of our competitive plans in Florida. I realized, upon reflection, how hard it was for me, mentally and emotionally, to be based in the highly competitive environment of that area of Ocala, and made a plan to rent in a different location the following year. I had to take a step back with Albert to help regain his trust in me and confidence in himself, and I made a promise to both of us to go at *our own pace*, regardless of how fast those around us seemed to be running.

In the interim, I participated in my first positive-reinforcement-focused clinic with former Sea World trainer Shawna Karrasch. The methods I learned were a real gamechanger for me in terms of deepening my understanding of animal behavior and expanding my toolbox to include a system that had been utilized with many species of animals for decades, but which had only very recently been more widely accepted in the equine world. I left Shawna's clinic inspired and excited to share my new discoveries with all my two-legged and four-legged clients. I was also fortunate to take on a client horse while in Florida that was appropriate for fulfilling my agreement to film online content for *Practical Horseman*. She and I spent a day with the crew, and I talked through the ways I introduced horses to cross-country obstacles on a long line before trying it under saddle.

I headed back north with a mixed bag of feelings at the end of that winter season. Things had wrapped up on a low note for Albert, which I felt a sense of embarrassment and failure about. I thought I should have caught the signs of his discomfort sooner and not have pushed him to a place where he lost confidence in order to fit in more competitions. All I could do was learn from my choices and do a better job for him in the coming competitive season up north.

I was, however, incredibly proud of the content I'd created with Noelle Floyd and *Practical Horseman*, and excited about the additional tools I had learned about in order to add them to my training toolbox. I had a feeling that the coming year in Maine would have even more opportunities in store for me, and I was ready to hit the ground running back at Unexpected Farm.

When we were back in April, I hosted Virginia Leary, the trainer I had ridden with growing up in Connecticut. Having her teach a clinic at my own farm was a full-circle experience; it was incredible to see her instructing my clients, as well as talk with her about training, one professional to another. It was fun to be able to offer Virginia ideas about groundwork and horsemanship training concepts that she was not very familiar with, and to have her later report back to me about her results when she gave them a try. My clients loved getting a glimpse of "where I'd come from" through Virginia, and seemed to appreciate having her unique eye for rider biomechanics assist them with achieving their own riding goals.

I also hosted my own "Basics of Positive Reinforcement" clinic, which was well-attended, as I was using positive reinforcement training in some way with almost every horse at the farm, with great success. It was proving to be an invaluable tool, especially with horses who had long-standing habits of behavior I was struggling to change. For example, I began using it to my school horse, Macaroany, use his body in a different way. It was clear by his upside-down neck muscles and "two men in a horse suit" appearance that Mac had never truly engaged his back properly in work. With positive reinforcement training from the ground, I was able to help Mac understand that movement with his head down, his neck stretched, and his back up was the place where he would get the most reward, both physically in his own body, and literally in the form of food when I clicked him for that posture.

Tik and Sinead came back to Wales for the second annual New England Spring Symposium in May of 2022. By that time, Albert felt more himself after his full round of ulcer treatment and time to settle back into his normal routine, so we were able to come to the experience from a more settled place than when we had left Ocala. Tik and Sinead helped me revise my competition plan for Albert, and did their very best to get everyone who rode that weekend off to a great start for the short Northeast eventing season.

Despite things feeling more "normal" with Albert during the Symposium, I was beginning to feel a flicker of doubt about his suitability for a career as an event horse past the Novice level. I tried to ignore the uncertainty, because I loved Albert very much, and I knew he was connected to me as well, but I couldn't help but wonder what his struggles might mean for us as a team, given my long-term goals.

Dan James was booked to come for a five-day clinic: two days of long-lining and three days of liberty work. Dan had been teaching at another facility in Maine for years, but it had been a primarily Western-discipline farm, so no one focused on English sports really knew about his work or how to access it. Having him at my farm opened new doors for both of us, bringing the English and Western communities in Maine together. I was finding that crossing traditional boundaries within the equine world brought me a unique joy that I had not expected, and I wanted to cultivate more such opportunities.

While Dan was at Unexpected Farm, I helped him with his horse, Applejack, giving him some pointers about his flatwork and imparting some jumping basics at his request. Dan also asked me to ride Applejack and the other horse he was traveling with, a sales project who needed experience out in the world. I played a bit with the sales horse bridleless, something I had been dabbling in with Albert as a way to break up more intensive workouts. Dan suggested I present a bridleless jumping demo at the 2023 International Liberty Festival in Lexington, Kentucky, an event that he and his wife organized as a showcase for the International Liberty Horse Association. He invited me to stay at his ranch. I was both surprised and flattered by the offer, which I knew I would take him up on, as it was another way to cross boundaries between disciplines and show people that good horsemanship is good horsemanship, whatever outfit the rider wears.

We rounded out the year of education at Unexpected Farm with Grand Prix dressage rider Lauren Sprieser. Caroline had introduced us, and Lauren and I hit it right off, despite our very different backgrounds. Lauren was fascinated with the concept of positive reinforcement training, especially for her more sensitive and spooky horses, and suggested that I come down to her farm the following summer to teach a clinic on that and other groundwork techniques. By the end of the weekend, Lauren had left my students and me with new ideas and exercises to up our dressage game, and I'd sent Lauren home with a few things to try out with her ponies. Through the often hilarious videos that Lauren sent of her experiments in the ideas I had given her, it was so fun to know she and her horses were embracing and thriving with concepts that were also actually moving them toward Lauren's upper-level competition goals. I was proud to be "spreading the good word" among top professionals in other disciplines.

In November, Albert and I headed to Equine Affaire once again, this time to ride with West Coast eventer and Olympian Gina Miles and natural horsemanship legend Pat Parrelli. I loved putting myself into these very different learning experiences each year to see where I might excel and where I could use improvement. Albert was foot-perfect in the clinics with Gina, and served as a shining example of readability and adjustability in the jumping exercises she assigned, but the brideless riding clinic with Pat, on the other hand, was humbling to say the least, especially given that Dan had proposed I demonstrate and teach about brideless techniques at the 2023 International Liberty Festival. It was a reminder to embrace the fact that I could be very good at *some* things, and still be a beginner at others, without that detracting from my overall worth as a professional.

While at Equine Affaire, I swung by the Trafalgar Square Books booth to say hi, as I had met the women behind the equestrian publishing company through Tik and Dan, who both had books published with them. Rebecca, the editor for the company, had been to my farm for the Laura Graves clinic, and she and I had hit it off as like-minded individuals in the horse world. As we were chatting in the book booth that Saturday afternoon, she offhandedly said to me, "Chelsea, let me know when you are ready to write your book." I made a confused face, not quite knowing how to respond, and then asked if she was being serious. She laughed and said she *was*, which somehow did not lessen my confusion.

Rebecca and I continued our conversation in a different direction, and I quietly filed a seed of an idea away as another possible unexpected opportunity, to be brought back out and examined—perhaps when I was on my long drive down to Florida at the end of December.

23
FINDING A NEW DANCE PARTNER

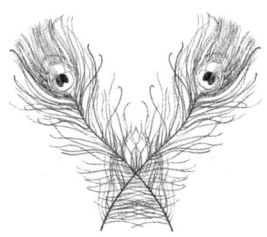

THREE CLIENTS, one working student, six horses, and I made our way down to Florida on the last day of 2022. Our destination was a wonderful private farm in Citra, owned by Donna Blem, who Tik and Sinead had introduced me to at the end of the prior season. I thought the facility might be ideal for me and my group—it was close enough to all the fun things that Ocala had to offer in the winter season but removed enough from the pressures of the typical competition-focused barns of the area. It was also less than ten minutes from Copperline Farm, Tik and Sinead's place, which made regular lessons with them easy to plan. This all meant that I was able to settle into my own routine and program with ease, including my "hopeful" competition plan for Albert, but I still had concerns he was not confident enough to move up to Training level, even after a very good season at Novice in New England the previous summer.

I talked with Tik and Sinead about my dilemma, and after watching Albert go in a few lessons, both agreed that pushing Albert to advance when he didn't feel ready would not be fun for either of us. This prompted me to *really* start thinking about what my options were with Albert. It boiled down to: keeping him and doing what Albert might be good at (possibly dressage or maybe working equitation), trying to move him up and seeing what happened (an idea that I didn't relish for his or my own emotional health), or selling him (which seemed like a very risky option for Albert's long-term well-being, as it would be easy to exploit his athleticism at the expense of his mental health). I talked through the issue further, with my clients in Florida and trusted confidants in Maine, and through much soul-searching, I landed on the fact that I wasn't ready to give up on my eventing desires, but Albert could *not* continue his beyond the Novice level. Our goals and path were no longer in alignment, so the best thing to do for him and for me was to find him a suitable home doing a different job than I wanted a horse to do.

A client of mine in Maine asked me to keep an eye out for a horse that would be appropriate for her to do some low-level eventing. I immediately thought of Albert, and I pitched her the idea. Alison was very surprised, and also flattered, and began to seriously consider my proposal. Albert, being the delicate flower he was, would have minimal disruption in his life. He would be able to stay at the farm he knew, in a program he was familiar with, and as Katie put it, "He wouldn't know who owned him, he would just know who loved him." He would just now have two people to love him instead of one.

With the excited assistance of my inner circle of clients and friends, and with my own trepidation, I allowed myself to begin looking at horses for sale in the Ocala area as I waited to hear back from Alison. Somehow, the stars aligned, and Alison decided to purchase Albert, which meant that he would stay at my farm, and I would be able to keep an active role in his training, helping Alison and him develop their own unique relationship. It was the absolute best-case scenario, and more than I could have hoped for. It freed me up emotionally to look for my next mount without guilt or anxiety over Albert's future, and it gave me some of the funding needed to look a new dance partner.

I tried several horses over the next few weeks, but none gave me that feeling I was looking for. I wanted simple. I wanted relaxed. I wanted uncomplicated. For years and years, I had been helping people with complicated horses and messy relationships, as well as managing my own emotionally fragile mounts. I just wanted a break from that. I wanted something that had "been there and done that," and that I could just have some fun with. My budget was meager in comparison to what the market was demanding at the time, so I had to look for something either green with potential but low miles, or lots of miles and some maintenance, but a history of reliability. I chose to focus on the latter, and it was like a breath of fresh air when I met Galicia ("Lila"). I knew right away, in the first five minutes of our first ride together, that she was the type of horse I had been looking for. I talked with my ever-supportive, long-suffering husband, made a plan for the financing of the mare, and somehow pulled it off at the end of February 2023.

As it is with a new mount, those first few weeks with Lila were not without their growing pains. It seemed she had not simply trotted or cantered over a pole on the ground in a long time, as she was surprisingly spooky about the process. She had a habit of getting quick toward show jumping fences, and scooting away from the landing sides of them, and she felt weak in her ability to carry herself on the flat. But she was the most fun ride I had experienced in years on a cross-country course. She was like a machine. Point and shoot. Safe and reliable and so much freaking fun. And she was *chill*. Lila gave off a Zen-like energy that instantly settled me. She had an ability to self-regulate that I had never seen in a horse. She could be a full-on giraffe, staring at something in the distance, and a moment later she would take a deep breath, lick and chew, and her lower lip would be drooping again. Her attitude toward life was inspirational and just what I needed. I could not believe I could call this magnificent animal *mine*. She was tall, elegant, and had a resume to be proud of. Ridden by US Eventing Team member Tamie Smith through Intermediate and around one Advanced event, with a history of wonderful care and ownership, Lila was an undamaged horse who I now had the privilege and challenge of getting to know.

How in the world did I get so lucky?

It was 2022 that really proved to me that *no one way is the right way*. At one time, I'd had a hard time going to clinics and learning new ideas, because then I'd feel like maybe I had been doing everything the *wrong* way, and I had to now revamp my entire process and align it with what I had just learned. I would get overwhelmed with all the tricks and exercises that I thought I had to incorporate daily if I was going to do it "right." For so long, I wanted to have a *single system* that worked. One I could follow and that would develop the kind of horses I wanted to be riding—predictable machines on an assembly line. But the more I began seeking new ideas simply for the pleasure of learning from horsemen and women whose work I admired, as well as taking in ideas from disciplines outside eventing, the more I could see the interconnected web of theories, concepts, and practices between them. I could see how the groundwork exercise a cowboy used would create softness in a horse that I would want in dressage, and how the "play" drive encouraged in liberty training with positive reinforcement could up a horse's engagement in jumping. I began to see how the depth and breadth of my toolbox was an asset that no singular system could encompass, and how my meandering path of personal growth was what allowed me to access that toolbox with the thoughtfulness, feel, and timing that I so admired in other professionals. If I had been simply striving to be seen and acknowledged as "good," *I would have never actually become good.*

It was an irony that was not lost on me.

When I purchased Lila, I'd had in the back of my mind that Dan had invited me to present about bridleless jumping at the International Liberty Festival in October of 2023, only seven months away. Albert had been a very reliable bridleless jumping mount, though he was prone to anxiety in travel and in "big" environments. I knew I needed to start bridleless work from scratch with Lila as soon as possible, as she had never been ridden without a bridle in her life.

At the outset of her bridleless training, I put a lot of pressure on myself to create a "finished" bridleless jumping horse before October, which in my mind looked like jumping an entire three-foot-plus course without a bridle. As our first few months in Maine together progressed, however, I realized that I needed to shift my goals with Lila. Not only did she start out as incredibly spooky in my indoor upon our return to Maine, which was all I had to ride in for many months of the year (even though I went south for the worst of winter), I also had competition goals with her. This meant there were many avenues of practice we needed to pursue in the months ahead—not just the Liberty Festival preparation.

From April to October of 2023, Lila and I worked at liberty once per week, jumped twice per week, and schooled on the flat twice per week. We did bridleless work on one of the two flatwork days, sometimes after a bit of schooling at other things, sometimes straight away. When I got her, Lila was very strong and flat in her approach to and leaving after jumps, which was much more easily managed in a bridle. It was a big learning curve for her to listen to my more subtle balancing aids without a bit in her mouth. She had to tune in to my seat, core, and sound cues so much more than she did in a bridle. She also had a lot more freedom of choice, as I had no way of keeping her head in an exact certain place. She could lower her head and look at whatever was in front of her, or crane her neck and head in any direction to look at things in the distance.

At first, it felt like Lila was somewhat disconcerted with the level of freedom bridleless riding presented, and she would spook and stop at very small jumps that caught her eye. At other times, it felt like she was absolutely loving her unobstructed movement through space, lips and ears flopping, forelock blowing in the breeze as she cantered along in her own lovely balance. It was an unexpected joy for me to be teaching a well-seasoned veteran something so new at her stage of life. Though I loved the prospect of taking Lila out and competing that summer, I loved exploring new places of learning with her just as much.

We spent the season competing at Training level, with hopes to move up to Modified at the end of the season. In New England, events are all between a two-and-a-half and five-hour drive away, so between helping clients, spending quality time with my family, and hosting clinics at my farm, I only got to about one event every four to five weeks between June and October. Lila and I won our first event. It felt like a win I could be proud of at that stage in our relationship.

The dressage was improving every time we went out, our show jumping was becoming more and more rideable, and even though she helped me more than I helped her on cross-country, it was our most confident phase together.

Our next event was much less successful, as that was when I discovered how much Lila disliked jumping out of mud. Though the dressage was consistently good, we had a very surprising stop at our first show jumping fence on course, and a harried round to follow, which just did not feel good to either of us. We recovered some confidence in cross-country, but I wondered if I had to be very careful about the venues where I chose to show Lila. It was likely that in her early career, she had not encountered mud, having run mostly in California and only recently in Kentucky. She had never experienced weather and footing like we had in New England.

At our next event, we scored an unprecedented "13.9" in the dressage (in eventing, the penalty score is determined by taking the percentage marks away from "100," so a lower score indicates a better performance). I was shocked, but I reveled in the score, jokingly writing to Tik, Sinead, and Lauren to ask if they might need any dressage lessons! But then Lila and I had multiple runouts in the show jumping warm-up, which took me by surprise. Though I knew exactly how I would coach someone to manage runouts, I blanked in the moment with Lila, as I was so caught off guard by her behavior. I did not do a good job making the wrong choice harder than the right one for her, and then I was hard on myself for the training mistake afterward. The competition round that followed the warm-up, though it had no stops, did not feel organized or smooth in any way, although thankfully the cross-country later did.

We still won that event handily, considering our dressage score, but not in the way I wanted it to feel, especially given show jumping had been my least-confident phase for as long as I could remember. I opted to stay at Training level for our next event, where I had originally hoped to move up to Modified. We were still having periodic stops and runouts at home when schooling jumps above Training level height.

One of my biggest struggles while in Maine for nine months of the year, then and now, is that I don't have regular coaching. Unexpected Farm hosts wonderful clinicians who I learn a lot from, but I don't have regular and consistent eyes on my work. So when things don't feel right, I don't have a trusted teacher there to help me figure out potential issues. With Lila, I did the things I knew I should do given her behavior and had her assessed by a sports medicine veterinarian in the late summer. After flexions and a look at her pre-purchase X-rays, we opted to inject her hocks. But that didn't solve the issue of the occasional—and to me, unpredictable—runouts.

I rode in a clinic with Olympian Boyd Martin after her hock injections, and at first, he wondered aloud why I was riding Lila a bit defensively. He encouraged me to get softer in my approach to the jumps, which I tried to do. Then he saw an out-of-the-blue runout when I softened just a hair more. From his vantage point, Boyd told me he felt confident it wasn't me that caused it, and he didn't think it was physical either. He suspected it was an old habit that Lila had formed long ago, and that I would simply need to always be on the lookout for it.

I talked to Tik about this new challenge, as well as connecting with Tamie about it. It was a real rollercoaster of emotions and fears, and I could feel my confidence dropping. In one moment I would think, *Maybe I am just not a good enough rider for this horse*, and in the next moment I would remember that not every match works, and that was okay. Tik reminded me of the latter more than once, and encouragingly said that he thought a big part of the issue was likely to do with how Lila was feeling physically on a particular day. I played with jumping her bridleless over some bigger jumps to make sure I wasn't contradicting with my "go" and "whoa" aids. Consistently, when the jump creeped up over three feet, Lila would look to say "no" by exiting, stage left.

In the midst of all this, Lila and I were prepping to be presenters at The International Liberty Festival, coming right up in October. My longtime student Morgan and her horse Ollie were coming with me to the Festival as a demo team for my clinics, and as my and Lila's partners in the night show, "The Evolution of Liberty," in which Dan had asked us to perform. We had a blast choreographing and preparing our act to music, choosing to use the Pink song "Trustfall," which seemed appropriate considering we were jumping without bridles.

Our horses traveled well to Dan's Kentucky farm two days ahead of the Festival, and had a great school in his ring before we headed over to the Alltech Arena at the Kentucky Horse Park in Lexington for the event. Lila was at first very overwhelmed by the atmosphere. I had never seen her so unable to settle. She grew about a hand whenever she left her stall, and I put a lot of time into groundwork and schooling rides in our first twenty-four hours there, trying to help her find her usual "Zen attitude" through familiar routines of work and play together. Because she was so "up," Lila and I basically walked the entire first clinic I taught on Friday, as she was too unsettled to do anything else without a bridle. Thankfully, I had long since let go of my assumption that I needed to show a "finished" bridleless jumping horse in my clinics, and instead I embraced the idea of showing a horse in progress. I was able to talk through my work with Lila, and my reasons for it, which was appreciated by the crowd watching. (Many people came to my booth afterward to tell me how much they liked how I highlighted my slow approach with Lila, taking into consideration what she emotionally could handle *in that moment*, rather than pressuring her into doing more.) Thankfully, Ollie and Morgan rose to the occasion and could demonstrate the more advanced concepts I was talking about.

By the end of my first clinic, I was able to trot and canter Lila around the huge arena bridleless, but I was nowhere near ready to jump her in there. In the back of my mind was the timeline: we had the "night show" rehearsal that evening, and the actual show the following night.

I used every self-centering tool I knew to work with Lila calmly and methodically in preparation for the rehearsal and show. I modified the height of the jumps, lowering them slightly, to keep things simpler for both of us, and spent a lot of time in the holding arena outside of the facility's coliseum, just hanging out with my mare while other horses came in, worked, and left. All the time and calm energy I put in paid off, and Lila slowly settled into the routine of work she was well familiar with. Our rehearsal went quite well, and I was relieved to be feeling much more prepared when I taught a second clinic with her the next day. We able to jump a good bit, which left me feeling pretty ready for our performance that night.

That performance…*that* show, with the cheering crowd, the music, the horses working with us and around each other, was the most fun I'd had in years. It was more fun than any competition I had been to with Lila, even the ones we'd won—maybe because there was no winning or losing, just entertaining others and enjoying ourselves. We reveled in the good time had by all when it was over. It felt very much like the theater productions I had been part of in high school. The camaraderie of performers, high on the adrenaline of making themselves vulnerable in front of a crowd, is a unique thing to experience, and I genuinely love it. When the Liberty Festival performance was over, all I could think about was how to find more opportunities to do it again!

Into the fall I wrestled with the question of whether my lack of desire to compete and move up the levels with Lila had to do with my lack of confidence with her in the show jumping, or with a real shift in my priorities and in the things I found brought me joy. It was impossible to understand that with total clarity because Lila was the horse I had—if I had a horse that could "take a joke" in the show jumping, and that I could make some mistakes on but would still jump, maybe I would want to be out competing and moving up the levels. Or maybe I really would just rather work with any horse I had on new concepts like liberty and bridleless work, or teaching to large crowds, than competing. This confusion left me wondering what my next steps should be with Lila and with my career in general.

I reached out to Marcy, my long-time mentor in The 3 Doors Academy, and had a couple of very helpful phone conversations over the course of a few months. The most poignant thing I remember from those talks was recognizing my own lack of acceptance of the parts of myself I deemed dangerous and untrustworthy from prior experiences in my life with horses. The part of me who was so tenacious and driven to win and be recognized that she became someone who overlooked her horses in the process was someone who I was always on guard against. She ate away at my confidence in little ways, and I was unknowingly exhausted by my efforts to keep her at bay. Marcy pointed out to me that, in fact, I owed a great deal of thanks to the driven part of myself. She was the one who'd begun my career with horses and who had motivated me to keep going when I felt like I couldn't. She had grit and strength and was a huge asset to my early professional life. The fact that she no longer served me in a useful way did not negate the fact that I could be grateful for her existence. It became my practice from then on to notice when I hardened against the competitive part of myself, take a deep breath, and say to that Chelsea, "Thank you. I've got this now," to "release" her from her "duties," and me from her influence.

I connected with Tamie again in the late fall, hoping for some further insight in regard to Lila. She kindly watched a few videos of me riding where the runout issue presented itself and pointed out several things that I should do to help Lila more. I was grateful Tamie took the time to offer her advice, but I left our conversation feeling like *if only I was a better rider*, I wouldn't be having problems with this experienced mare. I was feeling pretty defeated, slipping in and out of my old "not good enough" mindset, and reached out to Tik about it. He said he could absolutely see Tamie's points, but there needed to be some room for rider error in a horse that you are asking to jump big things, and that he still wondered if Lila was not feeling a hundred percent. He encouraged me to keep things simple until I got down to Florida where he could sit on her and feel things out.

24
FINDING WILDNESS

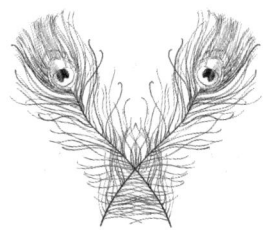

IN 2023, TIK HAD BEEN SELECTED to compete in Road to the Horse, a prestigious colt-starting competition in March of the following year. When we were chatting about his preparations, he mentioned that he was also interested in the Mustang Classic, a training competition that featured those preparing American Mustangs for English disciplines. Tik suggested that I should give it a go.

The more I looked into the idea, the more I liked it. The Classic was slated to be the first English-discipline version of a popular training competition called the Extreme Mustang Makeover, and competitors got a year to prepare. At the Kentucky Horse Park in September of 2024, wild horses and their rider partners would be asked to compete in a USDF Training level dressage test, jump a 2'3" show jumping course, and jump a 2'3" arena cross-country course. The top ten pairs then went head-to-head in a freestyle, vying for a piece of the $100,000 of prize money. That was more money than I'd ever had or would ever see at the kinds of events I competed in. The combination of training skills required to succeed at such a competition were those in which I knew I excelled. So I connected with two of my clients who were excited to back the proposed adventure, Alison and Michael, and I began my search for a Mustang.

It was much harder to get my hands on a competition-eligible Mustang when I lived all the way up in Maine, and it proved even more difficult when the relationship between the Bureau of Land Management (BLM), the federal arm that managed wild horse adoptions, and The Mustang Heritage Foundation, the nonprofit that ran Extreme Mustang Makeover events, changed right when the adoption window for the Mustang Classic opened. The flow of Mustangs to their usual adoption sites was altered considerably, and having never navigated that proccess before, I had a very hard time finding a horse. I had plans to travel to an adoption site that were scrapped because no horses were available there, and then turned to as many Mustang-related Facebook groups as I could to ask for help and direction.

A wonderful woman named Meg Magsig reached out to me via one of my posts and offered to scout a horse for me at the closest holding area to the East Coast, in Ewing, Illinois. Meg's farm just so happened to be a few hours north of Dan James's farm in Kentucky, where I planned to be for the Liberty Festival, so Meg and I made a plan: if she found a horse in the BLM holding pen in Ewing, she'd bring the Mustang back to her farm and put a few weeks of handling in before bringing the horse to me in Kentucky, and I would haul my new Mustang back to Maine with Ollie and Lila after the Festival ended.

The little six-year-old gray mare Meg and I chose came from the Twin Peaks Herd Management Area (HMA) in California, and had been in BLM holding pens for about a year. She had a big wide forehead and a curious expression that tracked Meg along the pen as she moved back and forth, looking at the options gathered behind the panels. She had a more petite athletic build than many Mustangs, so Meg thought she seemed more suited for English disciplines.

I called her Luna because of her white coat and the little half moon snip on her nose.

Meg began working with Luna twice a day, sending me innumerable updates and videos. She was of the same slow and steady, relationship-building mindset that I was, which made her very easy to relate to and have conversations with as she began Luna's gentling process. She described the gray mare as not the easiest—but not the hardest!—Mustang she had ever worked with. By the time she was to meet me in Kentucky, Meg admitted she had hoped to be further along than she was, but she felt confident in saying that taking her time with Luna early on would pay off in the end. I agreed with her fully and was so grateful that Luna got her start with such a caring and compassionate human.

I met Luna three days after the Liberty Festival ended, at Dan's farm in Kentucky. Meg backed her trailer up to a tall-sided wooden round pen and let the mare unload herself. We left her to settle for a while, and then Meg took her time to catch and halter Luna so I could touch her for the first time. The Mustang's wildness was still very much intact, and watching her navigate the human world all alone broke my heart. She was so genuine in her reactions to me and to everything around her. She hadn't asked to be there, without her herd or her freedom. She hadn't had a choice, and even though I knew she was better off with me than in so many other situations she might have landed in, I could not help but cry for her fate.

I had been around some amazingly well-bred horses in my life, ones with the presence of an Oscar-winning actor or Olympic athlete, but something about Luna awed me more than any of them ever had. It was her rawness. Her closeness to nature. Her trueness to herself and what she knew of the world, having really *lived* in it. She was the epitome of confident and "street smart," and yet she was trapped in a space of human creation. Now it was her time to become "book smart," and I could only hope I was up to the task of helping her.

I had never worked with a completely untouched horse before, let alone a wild horse. I learned quickly that there was a difference between a domestic-bred unhandled horse and one that had been living wild for the first six years of its life. *Everything* I did mattered to Luna. Every gesture, every breath, and especially every touch. Interestingly, inanimate objects were of no concern to her—sticks, flags, pool noodles, tarps, pedestals, jumps…anything that didn't have its own pulse was fine, as they weren't imbued with any meaning in her life. No one had ever told Luna that those objects were scary or that they were there to make her do something. She simply sniffed them, tasted them, stomped on them or over them, and moved on.

Allowing me to touch her was a different story, though. That took a lot of time and a lot of trust-building. I chose to use positive reinforcement with the little mare, which proved to be a very useful way to bring out her curiosity and trust, and also lit up her "seeking system"—she was a problem-solver extraordinaire, and once she knew what the right answer was from my clicker signal, she was on it and she didn't forget. We did most of our work at liberty the first couple of months, working on exposure to as many things as possible, especially since I knew that Luna would be making the journey to Florida with me in January. She would need to be trailered, stalled, and handled by multiple people on that trip, and I wanted her to be well-prepared.

I *loved* the blank slate aspect of working with Luna. Every new situation I encountered was a puzzle for *me* to solve in terms of how I would bring it to Luna as a puzzle for *her* to solve. I had to break things down into tiny steps and help her build understanding slowly. She would tell me if my steps were too big for her by getting frustrated and showing signs of anxiety in her expression and posture. She would find it hard to stand still, and her mouth would become very tight. She might pin her ears and try to give me answers that were correct for other questions, but not for the new one. It was up to me to slow down and think about how to make the question simpler. I had to find a way to break down the end result I wanted into smaller bites that Luna could process. When behaviors started to trend in a direction I didn't want, I could trace back through the work we had been doing to unwind and restart as needed. I wasn't managing someone else's prior mistakes and I didn't have to wonder where her behaviors were coming from. I knew where everything Luna believed about the human world had originated, which was simpler in many ways than trying to solve problems that had an unknown trigger or origin.

As with everything in my life, I didn't know what I didn't know about starting a Mustang. I tried to draw upon as many of the tools I possessed that I could imagine applied to starting a horse from scratch. Everything went amazingly well...until the day it didn't.

Luna and I had slowly progressed from desensitizing with saddle pad, surcingle, and bareback pad to working on the ground with an English saddle on, stirrups down, and girth done up. She'd never had any real worry about the girth. No "bronc" moments or explosive behavior. She watched everything I did carefully and seemed to understand that calm reactions were rewarded with food. She was a gem for the mounting and dismounting process, and though she lacked steering, she and I had done five short, successful rides at the walk in my indoor arena, with a few trot steps at the end of the last.

On our sixth ride, however, about two months into our work together, and just three days before our departure to Florida, Luna walked away from the mounting block when asked, as usual, but then picked up a little jog *without* my asking. I reflexively picked up the reins to slow her down, and the combination of pressures and sensations above, behind, around, and in front of her was just too much for her to reconcile.

Of course, I was in my indoor, as my round pen was outside, frozen solid, so Luna had a wide-open runway to pick up steam and buck. About eight seconds in, I did my best lawn dart impression over her head and into the dirt. My helmet did an excellent job of protecting my noggin but also came down on the bridge of my nose and broke it. I was incredibly lucky that it was the only damage done, as unpleasant as it was.

When I hit the ground, I saw my left contact lens pop out of my eye and into the dirt in front of me. And then I saw blood gushing from my nose. My very first thought when I got up, swearing to myself and trying to stop the bleeding, was, *But it was going so well!* I was heartbroken that things had taken this turn with Luna, and I felt like an absolute idiot for letting it happen. I had clearly missed steps in my process with Luna, and I was frustrated with myself for not even knowing what they were. I felt like I had been reading Luna well every day and that we had been making slow but appropriate gains in the right direction. Now it felt like there was a major setback, not only because I was injured, but because I didn't know what I needed to do to help Luna understand a rider without fear.

In the immediate aftermath of the fall, first at the emergency room and then back at home, I was also embarrassed. My face was a mess, and my confidence was once again shot. Half my thoughts were telling me that I was clearly not up to the task at hand, and the other half were reminding me that this was my first time ever starting a Mustang, and to cut myself a little slack.

When I reached out to people I trusted who I knew had experience starting Mustangs, they universally told me that this kind of thing happened to *everyone* at some point.

I am so fortunate that my personal learning journey has connected me with amazing horse trainers in the worlds of eventing, dressage, reining, cutting, Mustang and colt-starting, positive reinforcement, and liberty work. Even though I know it is literally impossible for any one person to hold all the knowledge that these combined individuals carry, sometimes I have a hard time admitting that there are things I still can't figure out myself if I just try hard enough. Reaching out when things go wrong isn't always easy for me.

I once read a Facebook post by classical dressage trainer Amy Skinner, in which she wrote, "As I tell my students often, I am critiquing the technique, *not* you as a person. So listen well, but don't smear it all over your heart because if you fail, it's a moment in time, not who you are as a person."

I had to remind myself of this message over and over again. Making a mistake or not knowing something didn't make me "bad" and there was no endpoint to the accumulation of knowledge that made anyone "good." It was all just learning, *not* a determination of self-worth.

The drive down to Florida three days after my fall was externally very uneventful, but internally very stressful. I did not want to be seen in public with my face as messed up as it was—two black eyes, a big cut across the bridge of my nose, and large scrapes in other places. I looked like a real mess, and I could feel myself retreating inward and hiding a little more every time someone noticed my condition or reacted to it. I wanted to crawl under a rock until I looked like *me* again. I recognized in that experience how much weight a person's appearance has, and how much I rely on mine when navigating the world. I rather liked my face, and people had told me that I was attractive throughout my life, so when that changed, even temporarily, it left me reeling. There were moments I could see the humor in my circumstance and would try to make up a good story about it, or when I could joke that any scars the ordeal left me with would be a reflection of my life story and only add character. But there were more times when my inner insecure teenage ruled me, and I would shrink away from being seen. The experience left me knowing I had some real internal work to do if I ever hoped to enjoy my life as my appearance inevitably changed with time.

25
FINDING CLARITY

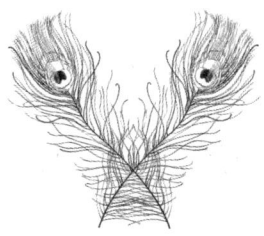

I REACHED OUT TO TIK about getting some hands-on help upon our arrival in Florida. Luna was at the right stage in her understanding to be great practice for Tik as he prepared for competing at Road to the Horse, and I knew I would benefit immensely from his help with the next steps of her training. Tik also rode Lila twice, and I scheduled his trusted equine sports medicine veterinarian, Angie Yates, out to the farm to give the mare a once-over.

Tik could feel the issue I had been feeling. The way he described it was that he had to be extremely accurate to a jump for Lila to feel confident. When he made what he called a one or two percent change in his body or contact on the way to a jump, she said, "No thank you," by leaving to the left of the fence. He also noticed as I had that if you got Lila more adrenalized by upping the energy of the work, you made it more likely that she would jump rather than run out, but in doing so, you also made it more difficult for her to keep her balance on the landing side of the obstacle. This had a snowball effect when stringing several jumps together, as the landing side of one would become the unbalanced approach to the next, and so on, until Lila would become more flat in the air, and therefore, more likely to start dropping rails. Tik and I agreed that this was a tough ride to have as an eventer when show jumping was your least confident phase, like it was mine.

When the vet came to see Lila, she found her to be in excellent health. She flexed every joint in the mare's limbs that she thought might cause discomfort when jumping and found nothing of note. She palpated her spine to no reaction, and outwardly could not see any reason why Lila might find it difficult to jump larger jumps. We talked about further diagnostic options and the benefits of following one path versus another. We talked about what the next steps might be if we found specific things, but it was all costly conjecture, as it so often is with horses. There was no clear, cut-and-dried answer, which made things even harder.

At least I could rest assured Lila was healthy and feeling good in her body.

As horse owners, we are faced with a lot of choices during our lifetimes: *Is it time to move up a level, or does my horse need more time where he is? Does my horse need to step down a level for his emotional or physical health? Should I move to a new barn for my or my horse's well-being? Do I need a new instructor? Do I need to call the vet or get a second opinion about this mysterious lameness?* And then there are the tough ones…like, *Is my horse right for me? Should I sell him?*

Any time I see a social media post scolding someone who has made the very hard decision to sell a horse, I feel immediately defensive of the person who had to make that decision. No one can know all the circumstances behind that choice—all the hours going back and forth, over and over the options and possible outcomes, the restless nights and guilt-ridden days, the curve balls that life may have thrown that made the decision for the individual. For anyone to simply assume that the decision to sell a horse is a selfish choice made without consideration of the horse's well-being is inexplicable to me.

Steve used to chide me when I would worry over a horse being sold to a new owner, asking me, "Who's to say that the horse's new owner won't take better care of him than his last one?" He would rightly wonder why humans assume that *they*, and only *they*, can take care of a horse in the best way and that anyone else will surely do a lesser job. I have thought of that often as I have taken in the many ways in which horses are cared for all over this world. I know how I think horses thrive best, and I also know there are people out there who would argue that their methods support horse health better than mine. Maybe we are both right...maybe the best rider match and daily routines that allow a horse to thrive can change over their lifetime. I know that to be true for the people who care for them.

These things were on my mind those first few weeks in Florida that season, as I wrestled with the decision of whether or not to sell Lila. After Tik's assessment, it seemed more clear that the mare and I weren't the best fit for each other in the show jumping phase of eventing. Thankfully, I knew with relative certainty that this was not due to any sort of medical issue, which ultimately, was great news. To me, it felt like the way Lila would need to be adrenalized and ridden to get the job done above Training level was not a way I felt confident or willing to ride, which was very hard to come to terms with. On some level, it felt like a personal failure. On a more rational level, I knew that *it happens*. Not every horse is a match for every rider, and it often takes time to figure that out. It's not right or wrong, good or bad...*it just is.*

Once I came to terms with the situation, I began carefully weighing my options. I did not feel in a hurry, especially because I loved Lila's personality and way of being so much. The way I saw it, I was back in a similar position to the one I had been a year before with Albert. I could keep Lila and pursue a dressage path, keep her and breed her, sell her as a lower-level event horse, or sell her as a dressage horse. After much soul-searching, I realized the bottom line for me was that I still was not done jumping, and I wanted to have a horse who willingly and confidently wanted to jump bigger things. It broke my heart that it wasn't Lila because I loved her so much for so many reasons, and it just plain sucked that I didn't have the money that would allow me to keep Lila just because I loved her, and also purchase my next eventing partner.

Thankfully, I knew that Lila was the kind of rare magical creature who would happily become the teacher that her next partner needed, and would inevitably settle into a new adventure with the grace and calm that she'd showed when she first came to me. Even with this understanding, I rode a rollercoaster of guilt, sadness, regret, second-guessing, and excitement for future possibilities. I kept riding it as I began to advertise Lila while keeping her in work and enjoying our time together. I kept riding it as I showed Lila to several people and beamed with pride as she embodied all the characteristics I described her as possessing. I rode it as I witnessed a young girl fall in love with her in the first five minutes of their time together, and as I got an offer from her family to purchase the mare. I rode it as she passed her pre-purchase exam and the offer became a wire transfer to my bank account, making the whole thing real.

I gave myself permission to spend my last two days with Lila riding bridleless, hacking, and simply enjoying the best part of what the mare had brought to my life: a sense of ease and calm. I cried at the thought of losing that reliable daily stability, knowing the respite it provided in my busy and sometimes chaotic life. I cried at the thought of Lila's confusion in being shipped off to a new farm with people and horses she didn't know. I told her how much I loved her, as I hugged her neck and felt both our hearts beating. I kissed her floppy lips and felt her breath on my face as I explained what was changing between us and where her life was heading. I got the sense that she understood me in some way, as she rested her head against my chest, and we stayed there together for a long while. The tears choked off my words as I loaded Lila onto the trailer destined for her new home with her new people, and they continued as I walked to Luna's paddock and cried into my Mustang's shoulder.

Lila was a reliable ground to my often windy mind, and a reflection of my best self. Letting go of her meant letting go of that touchstone. It meant that I would no longer have her to help me remember to breathe and slow down every day. It meant that I was more on my own to do the work of being the thermostat for those around me, the way that Lila had been for me, and that felt both frightening and depressing.

Selling Lila was a heavier loss than I had expected, even though I knew it was the right choice for her and for me. It felt like she and I had come together at slightly the wrong time in both our lives. If she had been younger and at the middle of her career, or I had been older and ready to slow my competitive aspirations down, the stars would have been aligned for us...but they were just a little off, and the reality of that was painful.

Change is hard, and as my mother used to love to tell me growing up, it is the only constant in this world. Whether it is change resulting from choices we make or choices that are made for us, it is simply part of the human experience. I had a hard time going with the flow when I was younger, and having a sense of control was what kept my anxiety at bay. It wasn't until I was an adult that I realized that my routines and need for structure, plans, and order in my life were my way of coping with anxiety. My habits and patterns were a set of learned coping skills that worked well for me, until life inevitably threw a wrench in the works and my best-laid plans had to change, like they did with Lila. In those moments, I would usually grasp at anything I could control and try to make a plan to get things back on track.

After years and years of laying those neural pathways in my brain, my default coping mechanism when I feel out of control is often still: make a plan, check things off lists, and regain control. Sometimes it works. Other times, not so much. Like when I have a horse that I thought would be one thing in my life and it turns out differently.

I now see two options in cases like these: I can keep trying to shove a round peg into a square hole and beat myself up mercilessly for not being able to "make it work," or I can get still, get quiet, and open myself to possibility, remembering that there is not right or wrong on the path of this life. I can either become defined by something I personally deem to be a failure, or I can see it as part of my journey, feel all the feelings and sensations that come along with it, and know that things will change again soon. Sometimes, "feeling all the feelings" takes longer than expected, or we think we are done feeling them, and then something touches a raw nerve, and we realize we are *not* done. It's easy to give others the heartfelt, empathetic advice to be gentle with yourself when traversing this kind of difficult terrain, but it is harder to follow the rule for yourself—or at least it is for me.

It is easy for me to look at the umbrella view of my privileged life, as someone who gets to play with horses for a living, has a beautiful farm, a loving husband, healthy children, and supportive family and friends, and to minimize my own feelings. I will often, uselessly, compare them to the larger problems of the world and its living beings, and feel guilty for ever complaining about anything. But those mental maneuvers don't change my nervous system. They can't talk my heart out of its heaviness or recalibrate my serotonin or dopamine levels. They usually only add to the confusion and guilt I am already feeling. So for me, I have to go back to the structure that provides me comfort, even though it doesn't provide any concrete answers. I have to go back to my meditation practice and the community of people I have built around me who are also "doing the work," and try to realign with the simple goodness of *allowing everything to be, just as it is,* even when it feels ugly.

Having Luna's forward journey paralleling my struggles with Lila gave a sense of direction and purpose to my time in Florida that season, which would normally have been filled with competitions and lessons advancing my riding skills. Instead, I learned more about colt-starting than I ever thought I would. I got to follow more of Amy Skinner's advice: "The sooner you can develop the ability to differentiate criticism about something you are doing from your self-value, the sooner you can learn and learn well."

While no one had blatantly criticized me for the work I had done with Luna, there was more than enough self-criticism along the way. But every day that I watched Tik work with Luna, I had the opportunity to recognize those critical voices for what they were—immaterial roadblocks to my own development. I got to consciously practice allowing them to dissolve back into the space they arose from and let them float away on the Florida breeze while I refocused on the daily journey of learning. I got to watch Tik prepare for Road to the Horse at several clinics with people considered to be horse training masters, which meant I was adding more tools to my theoretical toolbox.

Some clinicians showed me what to do, and others showed me what I would not ever do.

I realized that my tendency toward softness and fluidity that allowed me to work with very sensitive horses did not always offer me or them the opportunity to see what we would do when things got loud or messy. In my efforts to help Luna feel comfortable and at ease with the work she did with me, I hadn't exposed her to enough chaos or taught her about recovering from it gracefully. We had dipped our toes in, but we hadn't explored those depths to know how we would handle them together. I watched Tik press into those areas with my Mustang and help her come out on the other side, realizing that she was okay and that the human could still be trusted. She learned that sound and movement above and behind her were not a threat that meant she should flee the scene, which went completely against her base instincts.

My first couple of rides back on Luna definitely triggered a stress reaction in me, even though logically I knew she was in a more stable place. We were in a round pen, I was in a Western saddle and a rope halter, and Luna had been demonstrating a tolerance for being ridden that I had been able to watch and absorb. We had been working on bringing the energy up around her and then bringing it back down from the ground together, and her reactions were very consistent, trending in a predictable direction. But my heart still raced and my legs still felt a little like jelly when we started walking around the pen with me on her back, and especially when we took a few trot steps. My mind showed me images of the whole thing unraveling and me being thrown into a round pen panel as Luna spun quickly in the opposite direction and took off. I had to purposely take deep slow breaths to recenter and bring myself back to what was actually happening under me: Luna walking calmly around the inside of the pen. I also gave myself absolute permission to get off her if I felt she was building up to something, as I knew I would be no use to her learning process if she exploded again.

I let Tik take on many of her firsts over the following weeks: Her first canter under saddle, her first ride out of the round pen, her first trot poles with someone on board. Psychologically, seeing her do each new thing without incident gave me the confidence to try them with her. And just like everything else I had done with Luna, once she got something, she *had* it. I kept reinforcing her understanding with the clicker and treats, and the positive reinforcement clearly helped her understand new ideas and sensations more quickly.

Within a few weeks, we were venturing out of the round pen, walking, trotting, and cantering in open spaces, and even hopping over some small jumps. We took field trips to Copperline Farm for lessons, and to cross-country schooling spaces to play with water, ditches, and small jumps with me handling her from the ground. Luna was unfazed, even bold about these new obstacles. We stepped into a dressage arena without fear of the judge's booth or the sound of sand on the low panels at her feet. We walked into new barns and met new people without shying away. Luna had her feet trimmed for the first time, and then a second and third time. She had her teeth floated and her wolf teeth removed. She allowed me to clip her neck and shoulders without sedation, and she learned to get on and off a trailer like an old pro. We went to horse shows where I was coaching others and hung out on the edge of the warm-up arenas, taking in the atmosphere without worry. It was all really impressive, honestly, considering where Luna and I had been just a few months prior.

 I wanted to hang a sign around her neck to tell the world her story. I wanted people to know that she was a Mustang, and that everything I was doing with her was her first time doing it. I wanted people to understand why I was so excited that she hopped over a tiny jump in a new arena or walked calmly into a huge open field full of jumps and galloping horses. I felt so proud of her and how far we had come together, and I wanted others to share in the wonder of her progress. I also recognized a part of me that wanted to explain why I was riding a slightly downhill pony instead of a lovely, eye-catching, competition horse like Lila. That small part of me wondered what people thought of Luna, and if they assumed I was an amateur rather than a professional. That part of me stole some of the genuine joy the rest of me felt about Luna's progress, and I didn't like it. I tried not to fight it, as Marcy had coached me to, and to just observe it, and bring my focus back to the authenticity of my time with Luna. I tried to remember to thank that tenacious, competitive part of me for all she had done in my life—and then let her know that I wasn't in need of her services.

26
FINDING THE TAKEAWAY

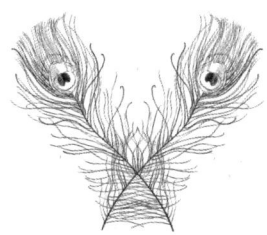

EVERY YEAR I GO TO FLORIDA, I count on learning things that have a profound impact on my understanding of and way of working with horses. There is usually some sort of epiphany that I feel shapes me as a professional and as a person.

As the first few months of 2024 passed, I waited patiently for the learning moment to be revealed, wondering when and where it would happen. As I neared the end of my three months in the South, I felt a little concerned there wouldn't be a big takeaway for the season, as it had been a very different experience than I had originally planned.

I flew from Orlando to Cincinnati to get to Road to the Horse, which was held each year at the Kentucky Horse Park in Lexington, Kentucky. I had offered to be part of Tik's "booth crew" at the event, and I had been preparing the setup for months with my students Morgan and Maddie, as well as some of Tik's team. The booth, where Tik would host meet-and-greets and sell merchandise, came together beautifully on the concourse overlooking the Alltech Arena. Maddie, Morgan, and I buzzed with excitement and nerves for what we were about to watch our friend do. For the prior three months, I had watched Tik prepare for this competition, knowing he had been working toward the event for an entire year. Luna had been part of that preparation.

I had seen Tik sink into self-doubt more than once during his year of study. After one particularly difficult clinic with a very experienced colt-starter, Tik had wondered aloud about his readiness for Road to the Horse, and I had told him that he was so much better than he thought he was. I encouraged him to just do what he always did—*be himself and be with the horse*.

There were four round pens set up in a big square in the Alltech Arena at The Kentucky Horse Park. The juxtaposition of what Tik did in that pen to what went on in the other three was like the difference between a symphony performance and that of a middle school band. I watched as the other three competitors immediately roped and pulled on their horses, trying to set a clear boundary about who was in control, while Tik befriended his horse. He showed his horse that he was the most comfortable thing in the pen for his horse by using impeccable observation, timing, and eventually touch. He did not rush. He never became frustrated. He was so palpably present in the space with himself and with his horse that I could barely take my eyes off the work. It was just like the first day I saw him teach at Equine Affaire in 2019.

When the first round was over, Tik had gotten further with his colt than anyone else and simultaneously had the most relaxed horse at the venue. His booth was mobbed with spectators, and as one of the three people running it, I had the privilege of hearing what visitors had to say. The common theme was that people had no idea what he was doing as he was doing it, but they could see the results. They didn't recognize his techniques, but they saw how his horse responded, and that was enough. They were mesmerized by his work, as I had been, and became instant fans. From young children to old cowboys, Tik had won them over simply by doing what he had set out to do from the beginning: *being aware of himself and the horse and nothing else.*

After three days of competition, and the ups and downs that come with working with horses, Tik also won Road to the Horse...by almost a hundred points.

And he didn't just *win*—he set a new precedent. In the words of one cowboy we met, "Everyone else here was in a colt-breaking contest. Your guy started a horse."

It felt to me like every heart in that space was blown open by what they had seen Tik do for three days, and as he was named the 2024 World Champion of Colt Starting, I sat high up on a panel, watching the stage, his family, and the crowd, sobbing and laughing, taking it all in. I stayed there for a long time, letting the feeling of that space fill me to overflowing with joy and love and connectedness.

I start crying every time I recollect it, and I think I always will.

As I processed Road to the Horse in the days following its conclusion, I remembered times in my own life when I'd started thinking about working with horses differently and seeing new concepts in action. I could never *unsee* the ideas or *unknow* the possibilities the new understandings opened up. Neither will anyone who witnessed what Tik did at Road to the Horse in 2024. They might not jump headlong into educating themselves like Tik or I did, but a pebble has been dropped in their ponds. The ripples are spreading, and who knows what each of them might shift and disrupt?

On my way home from the airport, I called Caroline. My emotions were raw, and part of me wanted to be alone, but part of me wanted to talk to someone about the experience. Caroline was one of the few people I could imagine talking to, because she knew Tik, and I was certain she had watched the livestream of the event.

At one point in our conversation, I admitted to Caroline that if I could do anything close to what Tik had just done at Road to the Horse when I competed with Luna at the Mustang Classic, I would feel like I had done something for horses in this world. Caroline very thoughtfully replied, "I hope this doesn't add any pressure to your preparations for September, but I want you to know that I believe in you as much as you believe in Tik."

I let Caroline's words wash over me and truly sink in. I could feel she truly meant what she said. Now, when I feel impatient at the pace of positive change in the horse world, I remember Caroline's words. I try to breathe into my heart and feel it expand against the contraction of my frustration. I try to remember that *everything I do* is impactful, though I may never see the outcome of that impact. My seeing it is not the important part. From being a part of Tik's team, to my own work with horses and people every day, I am also dropping pebbles into ponds, and I just have to trust that I am playing my part in the change I want to see in this world.

Before returning to Maine, I returned to the question of my next upper-level competition horse. I was feeling disheartened by the sales market in the United States, knowing how inflated it was, and knowing the finite nature of my budget. I knew that Sinead had been going overseas to look for her personal competition horses, so I asked her if she thought this would be a useful option for me.

Without hesitation, she gave me the contact information of her agent in Germany, Alexandra Von Beverfoerde, told me a bit about the process of importing, and gave me an idea of costs relative to purchasing a horse in North America.

Given my spending guidelines, it seemed that once again, I would either need to look for a horse on the younger, greener end of the spectrum, but with potential, or a horse on the older end of the spectrum, but possibly needing maintenance. Having just done the latter without success, I was more game to try the former, and told Alex this. In the coming weeks she began to send me videos of horses in Germany that might fit the bill. There were several that looked interesting, and once there were six horses on the list, it was time to make an actual plan to see them.

Up to that moment, when I actually began looking for plane tickets to Germany, the whole thing was just an idea. Almost a fantasy. On more than one occasion over the years, I had said that I would never be someone who could import a horse from another country. As I watched the videos Alex sent me and pondered actually going overseas to shop for horses, the impostor syndrome hit me hard. *Who are you to get a fancy horse from Germany? You are going to embarrass yourself over there, jumping horses in front of people who know what they are doing. You have no business doing this…*

Selling Lila had also hit me harder than I had expected. I missed her and the calm respite she'd brought to my daily routine far more than I thought I would. I thought I had given myself ample time to feel the heartache around Lila leaving my care, but I unexpectedly sank into a confusing depth of sadness that felt almost like an out-of-body experience in the months that followed. In retrospect, I can see that it wasn't just about Lila, but a convergence of big, emotional events in a short span of time. The accident with Luna, the change of plans with Lila, the journey to Road to the Horse with Tik and the profound experience there, was followed with an abrupt end of intensity when I got back to Maine, where I was welcomed by a late winter storm, accompanied by the loss of power for three days. I was overwhelmed with the guilt of being home with my family where I should have felt happy, but instead felt sad in a way I had not for decades. My mental health took a nosedive.

I wondered if I ever would feel any joy in competing again, and if there was a chance I wouldn't, why should I even bother getting an expensive, fancy horse, considering the many things in my life that needed both money and attention? At the same time, I kept making deliberate moves in the direction of going to Germany, as if that tenacious part of me I tried so hard to control knew better than my moving mind what would bring be back to myself.

I bought the plane tickets. I reserved the hotel rooms. And eventually I met Alexandra and her sister Louisa in Dusseldorf, Germany.

And then I met Flamant, a leggy chestnut gelding who instantly made me grin from ear to ear, the same way Lila had the first time I rode her.

He was the second horse I tried in Germany and instantly became the standard I compared every other horse there to. None of the seven others I looked at held a candle to him. He was light, soft, and keenly aware of his surroundings without being spooky. He had an uphill build that reminded me a lot of Lila, dressage-bred on his sire's side, and show jumping-bred on his dam's. I felt confident jumping him in an open field, and when we missed a distance or two, I never felt his confidence wavering to the next jump. I am sure the German onlookers wondered what the heck I was doing as I walked Flamant up to a ditch to see what he would do when allowed to study the question in front of him. He passed that test with flying colors, first looking at the ditch, then across it, then calmly hopping over it from a walk on a loose rein. I tried my best to keep a poker face but could not help but exclaim out loud, "He's so cool!" as we cantered past Alexandra, who was taking a video of us on her phone.

At the end of my whirlwind forty-eight-hour trip to Germany, I let Alex know that I wanted to go ahead with a pre-purchase exam on Flamant. It took place a week later, and because of the time difference between our countries, it took another few days to get a clear interpretation between the German veterinarian and my consulting vet in the United States. Much to my disappointment, the initial exam showed that Flamant had a significant cataract on his right eye. It was something that surprised his owner, as apparently it had not been present two years prior when he had purchased the horse. At first, I was convinced this meant my hopes were dashed and that I was back to the drawing board. I reached out to Sinead to get her take on the finding—in her eyes, there was a price point at which the risk was worth it. It was what I wanted to hear, as I had been considering throwing the owner a low-ball offer to see if he would take it.

After what seemed like an interminable wait following my offer, the owner came back with a counter-offer, and we settled on a price significantly less than he had originally been asking for Flamant. To me, the price felt worth the risk. My gut told me I was doing the right thing.

Flamant ("Fox") was only seven, giving me a sense of spaciousness from the get-go. There was no rush, no trying to beat the clock of an aging equine athlete to get out competing and moving up the levels. We could take our time, get to know each other, and move along at whatever pace was right. It was a low-pressure journey where I could regain that sense of groundedness in our daily sessions together. I was looking forward to beginning again, knowing my partner would be smart and big-hearted, and that we would carve our own path together.

27
FINDING ENOUGH

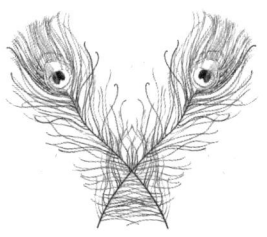

WHEN WE GOT BACK TO MAINE, Luna felt to me like a green pony, not a wild horse anymore. Now, she was something I understood more under saddle, and I felt more confident in helping her from the position of a rider. She settled right back into life in Maine, and we were able to get back to work under saddle a few days after the transition. I knew she would be my mount for the fourth annual New England Spring Symposium over my birthday weekend in May, so I was eager to make sure she was prepared to jump small courses by then. To that end, I planned to take her and one of my students with her horse to a local jumper show at the end of April.

First, though, I headed off to teach at Equine Affaire in Ohio, where I had been invited to present. It was during the heart of my Lila-related depression, and I was very lonely while there, missing my family terribly, having only just gotten home from Florida after being away for three months. I felt guilty for leaving them so soon after returning home to go off and do something I didn't really want to be doing at the time. But the talks I gave and the clinics I taught in Ohio were well received, and I was also able to meet some of the pillars of the Mustang community, including Stormy Mullins, Director of Events, and Matt Manroe, Executive Director of Mustang Champions.

It was wonderful to talk with them about their years of experience with the legendary breed I only knew through my limited experience with Luna. I left our conversation feeling even more excited for the Mustang Classic competition in September.

I was also able to connect the organizer of the Mustang Classic with Marco Baseggio, the head of Prestige Italia in America, and thus Prestige became the official saddle sponsor for the event. I felt the thrill of having been a part of connecting two very separate parts of the horse world, in hopes that they would both benefit and grow as a result of the resulting relationship, not only as businesses, but in understanding of each other and of horses. (I feel more and more, as I get older, that this is one of my most important roles in the horse world—making connections between people who might not otherwise meet and facilitating the cross-pollination of ideas that might help horses everywhere.)

I also was introduced to Western performance horse trainer Steve Lantvit, who allowed me to sit on his amazing red roan cutting horse, who politely escorted me into a pen of cattle and tried to do what I was asking him, while also clearly knowing that what I was asking him made absolutely no sense. That little taste of cutting piqued my interest, and by watching Steve teach a clinic afterward, I began to see the parallel lines between concepts and across equestrian disciplines that appear so often to me now. I could see how working a cow off a cutting horse is like starting a horse at liberty in a round pen. And how, in both cases, you have to be hyperfocused on lines of pressure and the eye of the horse or the cow to effectively predict its reactions and help it move in the intended direction. I felt that tiny spark of the love of learning in me once again, which gave me the distant sense that things would be okay. I just had to be patient and try to reconnect to my true nature, without Lila as my guide.

When I got back from Equine Affaire, it was time to take Luna to her very first show. I was incredibly nervous, as I had no idea how she would react to the atmosphere. I had only jumped her over a few jumps at a time in my indoor since getting home from Florida, never a full course, and I gave myself permission to call it a day if at any point I felt Luna getting overwhelmed. I wanted her first experience to be super positive.

That little gray Mustang blew my expectations out of the water that day. She navigated the show grounds carefully, but without overreacting, even when in close quarters with other horses and people. She won her flat class because she was the most relaxed horse in it, and even kept her cool when another horse went bucking by her as they were both cantering. She trotted over every rail, then jumped every cross-rail, and then did an entire 2' course at the canter, including a two-stride combination, which she had never seen before. She changed leads over fences and was adjustable between jumps. She stood quietly at the ringside when it wasn't her turn, and every time I left her with Katie to go coach a student, she would whinny loudly to me when she saw me coming back.

Luna made my heart so happy that day. I could not have been more proud of how far we had come together.

Luna was also a great sport at the Symposium a couple of weeks later, getting better with every session over the three days, and showing off how quickly she learned new concepts. It felt odd to be riding a pony at the event, rather than a more athletic mount like I was used to, but I had so much fun with her. She reminded me what it was like to ride when I was a child, carefree and low pressure, simply appreciative of the time a horse and I got to spend together. We dressed up, put our best feet forward, and truly enjoyed ourselves, which is something I know I forget to do in the hustle and bustle of my daily life and long-term goals.

We ventured out cross-country schooling soon after, and to our first rated event together in the weeks following the Symposium. Luna was unflappable. I felt safer and more relaxed on her in the chaos of the Beginner Novice cross-country warm up than I would have on any other horse in that arena.

I knew we would be ready for the Mustang Classic.

Even though all her new skills mean Luna is a little less wild, I can still see and feel her Mustang spirit. She still lives closer to knowing and trusting herself than any creature I have ever met, and I try to take time often to simply stand with her, heart to heart, and learn this from her. Even though I am still helping teach her about how to be a ridden horse, so that she can have a safe place to exist in the human world for as long as she is alive, she is continually teaching me how to remain authentic to myself. It is a gift I can never repay her for.

I still wonder often about my place in the horse world. My assumptions about it have morphed and changed so many times in my life, often through painful circumstances and difficult choices. In looking back, I can see that often these assumptions have been false, simply stories I've created in my mind and attached myself to through their telling and retelling. There was the story that my place was to "become someone" at the upper levels of eventing, and the story that if I didn't, I had failed as a human being. This story caused my intense drive to cloud my love for an animal who had brought me unparalleled joy in my life. Then there was the story that my only option was to remove horses from my life if I wanted to be a "good person." That story had to be proved wrong over a long period of time, with the consistent effort of self-reflection and the purposeful changing of habits. There is still the quiet underlying story that I need to define my place with horses completely and succinctly, like an elevator pitch, to be relevant in any real way, or taken seriously by anyone.

Beneath all these stories, there is the truth in the open space of simply *being*. That truth is that there is a deep, undeniable, unbreakable love in my soul for this other species, that I cannot define or explain through any story, no matter how well woven or eloquently written. It simply *is*. It is there when I strip everything else away. When I get quiet and still, it fills me up from the infinite space of my open heart, and I know it to be the truth. There is no story nor reason necessary to shore it up. When I am learning from horses or teaching other people about themselves through them, I am on my path, fulfilling my purpose in this lifetime.

And that is enough.

AFTERWORD
FINDING THE NEXT BEGINNING

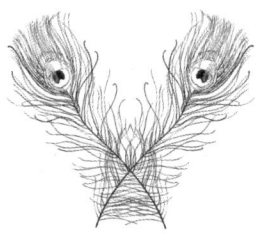

I HAD NOT BEEN SO NERVOUS for a horse show in twenty years. I think it was because so much was unknown. The Mustang Classic was an event that had never been run before and was being held at a venue farther from home than Luna and I had ventured since coming home from Florida. The atmosphere would be "bigger" and more intense than anything we'd yet faced together—$50,000 was going to the winner, and I was putting *a lot* of pressure on myself to "prove" something…and Luna was my very first Mustang.

I knew that many of the competitors had competed in the Extreme Mustang Makeover before, and honestly, I felt incredibly intimidated. I spoke with Tik the week before Luna and I left for Lexington, as he had participated in both the Thoroughbred Makeover, and more recently, Road to the Horse. I figured he would have a perspective that might calm my nerves a bit, and I was right. He outlined that usually in a group of competitors for this kind of competition, there would be about ten percent who, like me, were professionals who put in the necessary time with their horses, and who would be well-prepared and therefore competitive. Then there would be another eighty-five percent who would be a mixed bag of amateurs with varying results, but likely not in the top group of participants. And then there would be about five percent who would be borderline dangerous.

Our conversation definitely helped me feel a bit more confident, and after it, I made an internal commitment to the goals of staying open, meeting new people, learning, and hopefully making the top ten so Luna and I could perform the freestyle performance we had been working so hard on. I had to let go of the idea of "winning" if I was going to enjoy myself at all.

My longtime student and friend Morgan took time off of work to drive down to Kentucky with us and be my extra set of hands for the whole journey. Several of my students came from both Maine and from the southern United States. My mom, my daughter, and my right-hand organizer Katie flew in on Friday evening. And perhaps best of all, there was the total surprise appearance of Nick. I wish I could have seen the change in my exhausted face when I opened the hotel room door at eleven at night to see my husband standing there…I had not been so genuinely astonished since I was a child! For the three days of competition, I had all the support and good times I could have wished for—I received calls, texts, and emails with encouraging messages, and even friends and family who were not at all horsey cheered me on virtually. It was both heartening and uncomfortable to be the center of so much attention.

And then there was Luna, who tried her absolute heart out for me. In our schooling in the main outdoor arena on the Thursday before the competition began, I noticed that because Luna was small, I sometimes "scrunched" myself down on her so that I didn't feel like I looked like a giant on a pony. This habit didn't help the fact that she was already built a bit "downhill." I also realized that I was doing this when I looked around at other competitors and felt intimidated by them and how they appeared—the natural "uphill" build of some of the horses, and the willingness in their forward movement and softness in the bridle that sometimes Luna lacked. But shrinking never helps, so I resolved to ride Luna *as if* she was Fox—uphill and leggy with floaty gaits and a ton of presence.

On Friday, Luna and I had our best dressage test to date, landing us in ninth place out of fifty-eight teams after Day One. I had told everyone with me—who could all tell how nervous I was—that if I was in the top ten after the dressage phase, I would feel way more confident going into the jumping competitions. I was wrong. I was just as nervous as I had been for weeks!

The cross-country jumps were maximum height for USEA Starter Level and well-dressed, and I knew they would prove challenging to many of the horses there. I felt pretty confident that Luna would not care about them but went in riding like she might, just in case. I was glad I did, as she definitely took a hard look at a couple, but we were able to put in a clean round, landing us in fifth in the arena cross-country phase.

I knew that Luna had a super-cute jump in her when she was balanced, but she could also get a bit lax with her toes and take rails. My goal for the show jumping round was to go for "hunter-esque" and show off her lovely style while hopefully leaving all the rails up. We had one hard rub and one weird distance as Luna took some liberty with her pace toward the out-gate, but overall, I was absolutely thrilled with her performance, which gave us eighth place and secured our spot in the top ten, sending us on to the freestyle on Sunday.

I cannot adequately describe the combination of relief and excitement I felt at that point in the weekend. I could finally take a deep breath and let some of my nerves dissipate. I had achieved my goal of making it to the top ten—the rest was just gravy.

All the work I had put into my costume and freestyle preparation paid off, and Luna and I got to dress up like galactic princesses in shining silver and glimmering blues, with glitter on absolutely everything. I had planned the moon-themed act for months, complete with seven gleaming silver yoga balls of various sizes that Luna would push, weave through, circle around, and jump over. We were to perform to the Michael Buble version of the iconic song "Moondance," paying homage to Luna's name and the crescent-moon-shaped snip on the end of her nose. We turned heads and invited smiles as we wove, sparkly and bridleless, through the dressage show being held at the Horse Park between our stabling and the arena. I could tell that we both felt confident, having played a bit at liberty in the main arena that morning.

And then we got to the warm-up area….

There was a polo game being played on top of a hill in the distance beyond us, and Luna was transfixed by the galloping horses. I can only imagine that she saw a herd on the move as a signal of imminent danger, and her body immediately reflected that as she turned tense and distracted, totally unable to hear the basic cues I was giving her. I tried to connect with her for about five minutes in the neck rope before I asked Katie for Luna's bridle, sensing that I was getting nowhere fast and knowing I needed some help in guiding Luna's mind back to the task at hand. As Katie put on my Mustang's bridle, I was grateful that I had the presence of mind and flexibility to deviate from my original plan for our freestyle—something I would not likely have done several years prior. I began to think about what we could do in our performance if we couldn't go back to bridleless riding, while at the same time, methodically asking for transitions to help Luna settle and refocus on the communication between us.

Thankfully, my ability to focus on quiet basics worked. Luna began to breathe, and then to hear me again. After about fifteen minutes in the bridle, I felt I could go back to the neck rope. Luna was back, and I felt we were as ready as we'd ever be!

I never doubted that Luna would stay with me at liberty during our performance, even with all the space in the huge arena. I hadn't counted on the potential for huge props for the other competitors to be lined up along the fence (a truck "dressed" as a pirate boat, complete with masts and sails, plus a myriad of flapping and waving objects littering the ground, and even a twenty-foot-wide ball loomed just outside the arena), and those things did pull Luna's attention away from me during our lateral movements and Spanish walk. But even with those bobbles, I could not have been prouder when we finished.

Luna and I were third in the freestyle line-up, so I watched the seven performances after me. They were all fast and involved *lots* of props. They made our act look simple, and I feared *boring* in comparison. But no one else showed liberty circles or jumping at liberty, and I thought for sure those skills would bolster me in the standings.

Unfortunately, that was not the case, and upon reflection afterward, I could see that there was a kind of formula for the freestyles, and that a "wow" factor played more importantly than subtle horsemanship. In addition, one of the judges commented that she did not love Luna's expression during our act. Luna sometimes pinned her ears back when she was concentrating, which is a well-studied phenomenon in many horses as they are learning new things or doing more difficult work. I called it her "thinking face." But some might misinterpret her expression, and that was one of those things I simply could not control.

Sure, I wanted to place higher than ninth at the end of the competition, but I reminded myself that eleven months prior, Luna had been wild and untouchable. I had never started a horse from scratch before, let alone a *wild* horse. The others in the top ten had more experience than I did, and many of the horses were naturally more athletically built than Luna. What more could I ask for than what she had given me and what we had achieved together? My heart ached a bit, as the prize money would have made a huge difference to my family, but at the same time, it was bursting with pride for Luna and for myself.

Today, I trust Luna more than almost any domestic horse I have ever worked with, and I cannot imagine my life without her. She is the first horse I have ever had that I know I will *never* sell. She will be with me for her whole life, however long that is, reminding me what it is to live authentically, with my heart on my sleeve and my eyes wide open, taking in everything, every minute, the way she does, naturally. I will never get tired of her nickering to me when I call her name, or of hugging her for no reason other than it's *her*. I am so glad I took this journey with her, and that I now have a connection to an amazing mission-driven group of horse people who help organize and participate in Mustang training competitions. The

Mustang Classic felt different than competing for simply the sake of winning. It felt *purposeful*, and I can say for sure, someday, I will take that ride again.

ABOUT THE AUTHOR

CHELSEA CANEDY stands apart as a competitive rider who combines traditional training with natural horsemanship principles, groundwork, liberty work, and R+ training, and has a reputation as someone who understands how horses think and learn. For many years, Canedy worked in social service, and today she continues a regular meditation practice that she started over a decade ago. This firsthand experience in practical psychology and self-reflection underlines her ability to build the relationships with horse and rider needed to consistently improve performance.

Canedy has several Equestrian Masterclasses with Noelle Floyd, and she is a popular podcast guest, clinician, and presenter, appearing at festivals and expos around the country. Canedy and her family are currently based in Wales, Maine, on a beautiful historic property called Unexpected Farm, and she spends winters in Ocala, Florida (chelseacanedy.com).

ACKNOWLEDGMENTS

A DEEP AND SINCERE THANK YOU to every person who has been part of my story and of my ever-evolving community...that includes all the teachers and students I have ever had, and every horse owner who has sent a horse to me over my career, zero exceptions. You have all shaped me, and have brought me to where I am today—no regrets, only awe.

Thank you to my husband, Nick, who somehow loves this horse-crazy girl, despite the business and never-ending toils of our life together. I cannot imagine this ride with anyone else as my co-pilot.

Thank you to my children, Graesyn and Finnegan, for being my mirrors every day. You continually encourage me to reflect on my thoughts and actions simply by being yourselves. You are two of my greatest teachers in this life. Never forget, *you are enough* and worthy of all the love and happiness this world has to offer, *simply because you are*. And, you have the capacity to feel all of it—the joy *and* the pain that your lives will inevitably contain. It will not break you. It will shape you, and it will be beautiful.

Thank you to my mom, Joy, who is *always* there for me and my family, no matter what, no exceptions. I cannot fathom the depth of heartache your early years dealt you, and I am in awe of the way you move through your life, despite it. I am so proud to be your daughter.

Thank you to my stepfather, Jon. You are also *always* there for me and for my family, even though you are literally allergic to my life! I so appreciate our conversations about self-improvement and your dedication to that path in your own life. It is beyond admirable.

Thank you to my father, David, my stepmother, Kelly, and my half-brother, Reed. I know you are part of my cheering section, even from a distance.

Thank you, Steve, for sparking my love of learning new things about horses and myself by setting that example so beautifully.

Thank you, Nancy S., for your unwavering belief in me, from childhood to adulthood.

Thank you, Caroline S., for so gracefully supporting me and then allowing me to fall apart, even when it had a profound effect on your life. You are truly an inspiration in every sense of the word.

Thank you to Marcy and Gabriel, my 3 Doors mentors, for your tireless patience and kindness, your clarity, and your dedication to self-liberation. Thank you to my worldwide Three Doors family…I know that if I ever need the support of any one of you, you will be